THE 101 BEST

Marine Invertebrates

THE ADVENTUROUS AQUARIST™ GUIDE SERIES

Produced and distributed by:

T.F.H. Publications, Inc.
One T.F.H. Plaza
Third and Union Avenues
Neptune City, NJ 07753
www.tfh.com

Copyright © 2008 by T.F.H. Publications, Inc.

All rights reserved. No part of this publication may be reproduced, stored, or transmitted in any form, or by any means electronic, mechanical, or otherwise, without written permission from the publisher, except where permitted by law. Requests for permission or further information should be directed to the above address.

Printed and bound in China
08 09 10 11 12   1 3 5 7 9 8 6 4 2

ISBN-13: 978-1-890087-23-4
ISBN-10: 1-890087-23-8
UPC-A: 6-81290-08723-2

Library of Congress Cataloging-in-Publication Data
Michael, Scott W.
1961–
Marine invertebrates : how to choose and keep hardy, brilliant, fascinating species that will thrive in your home aquarium / by Scott W. Michael; photography by Janine Cairns-Michael ... [et al.].
p. cm. -- (The adventurous aquarist guide series; 4)
Includes bibliographical references and index.
ISBN 1-890087-23-8
1. Captive marine invertebrates. I. Title.
SF457.1.M526 2008
639'.4--dc22   2008007823

Color by Digital Engine
Designed by Linda Provost

A MICROCOSM/TFH Professional Series Book

TFH Publications, Inc.
Neptune City, NJ 07753
www.tfh.com

Microcosm, Ltd.
Charlotte, VT 05445
www.microcosm-books.com

THE 101 BEST

Marine Invertebrates

HOW TO CHOOSE & KEEP HARDY, BRILLIANT, FASCINATING SPECIES THAT WILL THRIVE IN YOUR HOME AQUARIUM

Text & Principal Photography
Scott W. Michael

MICROCOSM

tfh

PROFESSIONAL
SERIES™

A Microcosm Edition

WWW.MICROCOSM-BOOKS.COM

Front Cover

Fire Shrimp (*Lysmata debelius*), page 136;
photograph by Matthew L. Wittenrich

Back Cover

Top: Zoanthids (*Zoanthus* sp.), pages 62–67; Matthew L. Wittenrich

Middle: Basic Invertebrate Aquarium Care, page 18; Matthew L. Wittenrich

Bottom: Electric Orange Hermit Crab (*Calcinus* sp.),
page 127; Scott W. Michael

DEDICATION

To my Uncle Bert Homan,

whose optimistic outlook on life

and honorable character is something

I strive to emulate.

Thank you for your frequent encouragement,

Bert, and your long service

to the defense of our freedom.

ACKNOWLEDGEMENTS

Many professional aquarists, committed home aquarists and marine livestock wholesalers have assisted me greatly over the years and in preparing this book. I express immense gratitude to the following: Bill Addison, Chris Buerner, and Bob Pascua (Quality Marine), Mitch Carl (Henry Doorly Zoo), Dr. Bruce Carlson (Georgia Aquarium), Millie, Ted, and Edwin Chua (All Seas Marine), Carl Coloian (Sea Dwelling Creatures), J. Charles Delbeek (Waikiki Aquarium), Dustin Dorton and Jim Norris (Oceans, Reefs and Aquariums), Tom Frakes, Kevin Gaines, Mark Haeffner (Fish Store Inc.), Richard Harker, Jay Hemdal, Larry Jackson, Kelly Jedlicki, Kevin Kohen (liveaquaria.com), Morgan Lidster (Inland Aquatics), Chandra Liem (Golden Generation), Martin A. Moe, Jr., Bronson Nagareda, Michael S. Paletta, Richard Pyle, Vince Rado (Segrest Farms), Dennis and Erik Reynolds (Aqua Marines), Mike Schied, Frank Schneidewind, Terry Siegel (Advanced Aquarist Online), Julian Sprung (Two Little Fishies), Wayne Sugiyama (Wayne's Ocean World), Leng Sy (Ecosystem Aquariums), Dr. Hiroyuki Tanaka, Takamosa and Miki Tonozuka (Dive and Dives), Jeffrey Turner (Reef Aquaria Design), Jeff Voet (Tropical Fish World), Tony Wagner (CaribSea), Fenton Walsh, Jim Walters (Old Town Aquarium) and Forrest Young and Angus Barnhart (Dynasty Marine Associates). For their contributions of photography, I am very grateful to Alf Jacob Nilsen (Bioquatic Photo), Matt Wittenrich, Paul Humann, Denise Nielsen Tackett, Bob Fenner, and Dave Burr at Vivid Aquariums. I am extremely appreciative of the work of the Microcosm publishing team, especially Linda Provost, Janice Heilmann, John Sweeney, Mary E. Sweeney, Emily Stetson, Judith Billard, and Editor James Lawrence. Thanks also to the folks at T.F.H. Publications, especially Glen Axelrod, Mark Johnson, and Chris Reggio for helping this effort come to fruition. I am especially indebted to my American and my New Zealand family for their support over the years. Anyone who knows me, knows that Janine Cairns-Michael, my wonderful spouse, is a saint who puts up with my obsessive-compulsive tendencies. Her never-failing support for nearly a quarter of a century has been essential for much of what I have achieved in my life.

—Scott W. Michael
Lincoln, Nebraska

CONTENTS

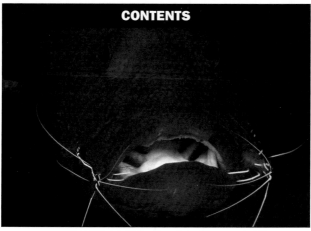

Pair of Scarlet Cleaner Shrimp grooming a grouper, page 141.

CONTENTS

Invertebrates to Avoid

Model Invertebrate Communities

Quick Invertebrate Finders .... Inside Covers

Meant as a field guide to marine aquarium invertebrate groups and species, this guide uses color photographs taken in home aquariums as well as on coral reefs for quick visual identification. Species appearing here have been selected as outstanding for their hardiness and durability in aquarium conditions, for their attractiveness, and for their interesting behaviors.

Invertebrates are arranged in taxonomic order, generally from those with simpler anatomies to those with increasingly complex body forms. Within these phyla or classes, species are presented alphabetically by common name within their organism groupings.

Subheadings within each species account contain concise reference material, advice, and comments organized as follows:

COMMON NAME

In this guide one or more common names are listed for each species. The first name provided is the name most frequently used in the authoritative checklists and field guides written by invertebrate zoologists. In assigning the preferred common name to each species, I have attempted to steer away from obvious misnomers and toward names that will minimize confusion and bring science and hobby closer together.

SCIENTIFIC NAME

This is the most-current name applied to the organism by the scientific community. The name is in the form of a binomial. The first name indicates the genus to which the animal or plant belongs, while the second is the species name. When common names are confusing, the scientific name is a benchmark that all can understand. For example, *Condylactis gigantea* is the scientific name for a popular sea anemone that goes by all of these common names: Caribbean Giant Anemone, Florida Pink-tipped Anemone, Haitian Anemone, Condy, and others. The genus name often provides a clue to the traits and keeping requirements of other closely related species grouped within that genus.

NATIVE RANGE

This entry notes the broad geographical area where each species occurs. The distribution of an animal is of great value to aquarists wishing to set up a tank replicating a natural community or biotope of fishes and invertebrates from a certain geographical region.

MAXIMUM SIZE

This usually indicates the greatest height or diameter that an individual of that particular species typically attains. Unlike most reef fishes, marine invertebrates can live for many decades or even centuries in the case of coral colonies, and sizes of mature animals vary considerably. In most cases, the size of an aquarium specimen will fall short of the size listed, but the aquarist should always note the adult sizes of prospective purchases.

MINIMUM AQUARIUM SIZE

This is the minimum suitable aquarium volume for an adult individual of the species, with the exception of corals, which can outgrow even large systems but that may be pruned or fragmented from time to time. This is the minimum suitable size; providing more space will usually allow any invertebrate to acclimate better, display less aggression toward its tankmates, and make for easier maintenance of good water quality.

LIGHTING

Light is essential for the growth and survival of most invertebrates. Even those that are not photosynthetic usually need at least moderate lighting to elicit normal daily behaviors and to foster the growth of algae for grazing. "Bright light" in an aquarium is usually in the range of 5-8 watts/gallon, and usually calls for power compact fluorescent, T5 bulbs, or metal halide bulbs. "Moderate lighting" (3-4 watts/gallon) can be provided by an array of fluorescent bulbs or power compact bulbs.

WATER

Correct and safe water temperature for most coral reef animals is in the range of 75-82° Fahrenheit or 24-28° Celsius.

FEEDING

Marine animals vary dramatically in their feeding preferences and requirements. Those that derive energy from the photosynthesis carried on by their symbiotic zooxanthellae (page 24) are noted. Suggestions are given for a variety of acceptable food types, and a feeding frequency is recommended.

See pages 31–36 for specific foods and feeding advice.

AQUARIUM COMPATIBILITY

Behaviors (and feeding habits) that make a particular species better or less well suited to keeping with other aquarium species are noted here. "Reef safe" usually applies to species that will not eat coral polyps, anemones, or clams.

COLOR KEY TO AQUARIUM SIZE

One of the most important criteria for the selection of an invertebrate is its eventual adult size. Will it fit in your aquarium? That beautiful baby *Tridacna gigas* clam may not be the best choice for your new nano reef. Here is the Size Key used in this guide:

SMALL (or NANO):
Requires minimum aquarium size of 10–30 gal. (38–114 L)

MEDIUM:
Requires minimum aquarium size of 50–75 gal. (190–285 L)

LARGE:
Requires minimum aquarium size of 100–180 gal. (380–684 L)

Spineless wonders
of the reef
A primer for moving successfully
from a fish-only tank to a reef aquarium

If you've ever had the great fortune to put your mask-clad face beneath the water's surface on a coral reef, you were no doubt astonished by the dramatic scene before you.

Two things struck me the first time I had this opportunity—the incredible colors and the diversity of life forms. Brilliantly hued fishes "played" among the earth-toned soft and stony corals. There was also an occasional coral colony whose chromatic characteristics caused it to stand out from its more muted neighbors. Some of these were flaming red, hot pink, bright yellow, or vivid purple. There were colorful, flowerlike sea anemones that provided a home to cheeky anemonefishes. Some of the invertebrate life was not so obvious. Upon closer inspection I found that the reef's caves and crevices were veneered with colorful sponges and tunicates—a living carpet where resident shrimps and crabs could find food and shelter. So much color and so much life! I believe it is these two alluring aspects of coral reefs that draw most of us into the marine aquarium hobby.

As appealing as the fishes are, it is the profusion of invertebrate life that one finds on coral reefs that really sets this ecosystem apart from freshwater environments.

Invertebrates—"inverts" for short—are classified as animals that lack a backbone or spinal cord. While there are tropical freshwater ecosystems that boast diverse fish communities (think of the myriad species from the Amazon River and Africa's Rift Lakes), relatively few invertebrate phyla are available to the freshwater aquarium keeper. In a reef aquarium, it is possible to acquire and keep living representatives from at least eight different invert phyla: sponges, corals, mollusks, segmented worms, arthropods/crustaceans, echinoderms, bryozoans, and tunicates. Members of other phyla also routinely arrive in marine aquariums as hitchhikers on live rock, in live sand, and hiding on coral colonies.

Reef invertebrates range in appearance from the familiar to

*Two beautiful and relatively easy-to-keep invertebrates: a Caribbean Giant Anemone (*Condylactis gigantea*) and its commensal* Periclimenes *shrimp.*

13

the bizarre and in size from microscopic to massive coral colonies weighing many tons. (The largest animal-made structure on earth is the Great Barrier Reef, 1,250 miles of majestic mass easily visible from space, entirely built by marine invertebrates.)

Invertebrates also vary dramatically in color. Some are as brightly pigmented as their most ostentatious fish-neighbors, while others sport pigments that help them to disappear against more muted surroundings. While their fantastic forms and striking colors are enough to make these animals worthy of aquarium display, the behavioral repertoire of some species increases their appeal.

Consider the shrimp species that act as groomers, plucking small parasites and dead tissue off sick or wounded fishes that seek them out to take advantage of these beneficial services. How about the shrimps that live in communion with bottom-dwelling gobies—the shrimp digs a burrow in which the happy couple live, while the goby acts as a sentinel, warning its crustacean partner when danger is near.

The classic invert-fish partnership that exists between sea anemones and certain fishes (namely the anemonefishes or clown-

Invertebrates for sale: choices of marine livestock in a good local fish store can be incredibly varied—and confusing—for newcomers to reefkeeping.

fishes) can make for a fascinating display. Keeping the anemone alive and healthy in captivity has long been the challenge of replicating this symbiotic relationship in the aquarium. As discussed elsewhere in these pages, choosing the right species of anemone and feeding it properly can go a long way to assuring your success.

Then there are the octopuses, the Einsteins of the invertebrate world, which exhibit an incredible aptitude to learn and solve problems. For the aquarist with some experience and the willingness to dedicate a tank and special care to one of these animals, an octopus can become a fascinating pet.

Many other invertebrates exhibit interesting and unusual feeding behaviors that can add greatly to the interest and biological balance of a marine aquarium. Some can aid the aquarist in cleaning chores. These include snails that feed on pestilent algae, hermit crabs that consume leftover food, shrimps that attack nuisance *Aiptasia* anemones, sea cucumbers that mop up accumulating detritus, and brittlestars that prevent uneaten food from polluting the aquarium.

There are now many hundreds of "spineless" marine animals

available in the aquarium trade, with new species appearing all the time. This invert boom coincides with a surge in popularity of the reef aquarium (defined as a vessel in which the aquarist maintains various invertebrate inhabitants, the focal point of which is usually a rich coral community).

For the aquarist who has come through the usual progression from a freshwater aquarium to a basic saltwater fish-only system now to the verge of keeping invertebrates, we hope this guide will help ensure your success. This book provides an introduction to many interesting invertebrates that can easily be kept in a fish-and-hardy-invertebrates aquarium, provided that some minimal husbandry standards are met and that copper and other medications are kept out of the system.

A full-blown reef aquarium, of course, requires enhanced equipment and husbandry techniques. For those ready to upgrade their lighting and circulation, and to pay more attention to filtration and water quality, a whole new world of colorful, exotic invertebrate species awaits.

However, all the best reef gear and the most pristine water

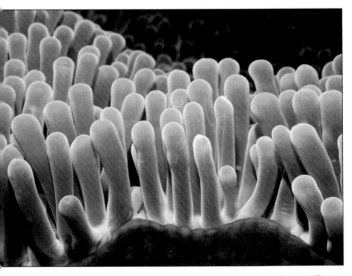

*One to avoid: the Magnificent Sea Anemone (*Heteractis magnifica*) is difficult to keep in captivity and should be reserved for experts or left in the sea.*

Better choice: The Bubble-tip Sea Anemone is an ideal choice for the aquarist who hopes to replicate the anemone-anemonefish symbiotic relationship.

conditions in the world will not compensate for the hobbyist who stocks the wrong animals in his or her system.

Unfortunately, not all invertebrates are created equal when it comes to their ease of care and their survival rates in captivity. Some can bring havoc into your aquarium, others demand expert care to survive, and some that are routinely sold to hobbyists have the ability to sting, bite, and even kill human beings.

How do you know which of the many species available are suitable for your system and your skill set as a marine aquarium keeper?

In this book, I have tried to highlight the commonly available invertebrates that fare best in captivity. While some of these animals have special needs, these are all relatively easy to meet with a little planning and regular maintenance.

In the Invertebrates to Avoid section, we highlight some invertebrates that are difficult to keep alive, potentially dangerous to their keepers, or destructive in a captive community. We have also provided a number of model aquarium communities built around the included invert species to inspire the hobbyist ready to move beyond a fish-only tank and into the realm of the reef aquarium.

Motion in the ocean:
The importance of water movement

If you have ever been snorkeling or scuba diving on a coral reef, you know that the water is anything but calm or stagnant. There can be wave action, surge, tidal flows, oceanic currents, and more. While diving, I have been on reef faces that were lush with luxuriant growths of both stony and soft corals and where the water motion was so strong I was "waving" in the current like a flag in a 20-knot wind while secured to a dead portion of the rocky substrate with a hook and 4-foot rope (a.k.a. a "reef hook").

Water motion in the ocean has impacted how coral reef animals have evolved, especially those that lead a stationary or sessile lifestyle. (Fishes and inverts that move are known as "motile.") Every animal has a layer of water around it called the boundary layer. It is a thin layer of stagnant water that creates a potential barrier to the uptake and release of oxygen, trace elements, and other substances. A sessile invertebrate that is not subjected to vigorous water movement will have a thicker boundary layer than one that is being constantly "flushed." Therefore, it is important to produce enough water movement around a sessile invertebrate to prevent this boundary layer from becoming even more impenetrable to gas and nutrient exchange.

In the case of sedentary animals that produce mucus, water movement also serves to prevent an over-abundance of slime from building up around the organism. Some corals produce amazing amounts of mucus when they're stressed. (There is one beautiful *Acropora* coral commonly known as the "Bali Slimer" because of its habit of coating itself in a smelly goo when it is disturbed.) It is possible that if such a coral colony is not subjected to enough current, it could suffocate in its own slime. (A practical tip—if you have a coral that is producing excessive mucus, make sure it is in a current-prone part of the aquarium and occasionally blast it with water expelled from a turkey baster or a powerhead.)

Water movement also "cleans" sedentary animals of fecal material and sediment that may land on them. Detritus that accumulates

A lush coral garden: essential environmental conditions include crystal-clear water, low nutrient levels, bright lighting, and vigorous, chaotic water motion.

among the polyps of encrusting soft corals and sponges can act as a fertilizer and will encourage pest algae to overgrow these animals.

Currents also bring food to animals that rely on suspension/filter feeding. Once again, this is especially true for inverts like corals, feather duster worms, clams, scallops, and certain sea stars, serpent stars, and sea cucumbers. Many marine fishes also benefit from good currents—but for sessile invertebrates, adequate water motion is absolutely essential.

MAKING WAVES

Once you know that current is important, how do you create it in your aquarium? First, let's think about what sort of circulation we want.

Water movement can be classified into one of three categories: laminar flow (steady and unidirectional), surge (unidirectional pulses of strong and weak flow), and turbulence (random, multidirectional flow). Of these three, the most desirable, and also the most difficult to recreate in the aquarium, is turbulence. Because it is multidirectional, it is more likely to reduce the boundary layers around more of the animal's body surface.

Water movement in a fish-only tank is typically achieved with a water pump that returns water from the sump or external power filter to the display tank. Many marine aquarists now also routinely add powerheads to provide currents to their tanks. Powerheads can be very affordable sources of current and can be directed toward specific areas of the tank that may otherwise have limited water flow. There are oscillating powerheads that rotate so that they direct water flow over a larger area. The downside of these pumps is they produce heat. However, if you have the budget (they are expensive), there are powerheads that have an external motor that transfers torque, via an electric field, through the aquarium glass to a propeller in the tank. In this way, heat transfer is avoided. When using powerheads in the aquarium, you need to ensure that there is a barrier over the intake opening of the pump so animals are not sucked into the impeller and injured or killed.

Most powerheads and circulating pumps produce laminar flow (though as mentioned previously, some rotate to direct the flow over a larger area). In order to get a more turbulent effect, reef aquarists

A new generation of powerheads allows aquariums large and small to have more appropriate, turbulent currents, especially if two or more units are used and controlled by a wavemaker that randomly switches them on and off.

often use timers so that one or more powerheads go on and off intermittently—these are often referred to as wavemakers and are now available in all price ranges. They are a good investment.

So how much water motion do we need in our tank? This is, of course, dependent on the animals you intend to keep. If you are interested in keeping corals and sea anemones, one powerhead with flow rate of 500 or more gallons per hour for every 2 feet of tank length is a good recommendation. (For a standard 75-gallon tank, two powerheads are needed.) Another rule of thumb is to have a total flow rate of 20 times the water volume of the aquarium. (For a 75-gallon tank that would be 1,500 gallons, so you might use two powerheads rated at 750 or 850 gph.)

Some sessile invertebrates prefer less vigorous water movement. Some of the large-polyped corals and mushroom anemones may not do as well if pounded directly by water flow from a standard powerhead. These animals should be placed in a part of the tank with less water agitation. Some of the newer powerheads without small-diameter nozzles expel water in a broader, more "gentle" stream—these are less likely to cause mechanical damage to more delicate corals. Water flow will also impact the growth forms of sessile invertebrates and may even inhibit growth if it is too strong.

Elementary water chemistry

If you happen to love chemistry, a marine aquarium and all the water-testing paraphernalia available can provide a lifetime of delight and mental challenges. For the rest of us who lack fond memories of chemistry class, the good news is that we do not need to become chemists or memorize formulas to successfully keep an invertebrate or reef aquarium. However, there are some basic tests and a few water parameters you must keep an eye on to ensure that your inverts stay healthy.

SALT CONTENT

Marine aquarists, from beginners to professionals, all need to monitor the salt content in their aquarium water. This becomes more important with many invertebrates, which tend to be more sensitive to salinity changes. Salinity is a measure of the quantity of salts that are dissolved in the water. It tends to drift over time in an aquarium, with the impacts of evaporation, water changes, and loss of salt to crusts. Most hobbyists measure the salt content of

The tiny Sexy Shrimp (Thor amboinensis) is a wonderful animal for smaller tanks but is very sensitive to abrupt changes of salinity or pH.

water by checking the specific gravity with an instrument called a hydrometer or salinometer. An acceptable specific gravity for the water in your invertebrate aquarium would be 1.023 to 1.026. (If using a saltwater refractometer, a more expensive and more accurate instrument, the salinity reading should be 34 to 35 ppt to match natural seawater.) Some invertebrates can be mortally sensitive to abrupt changes of salinity, and some will go into decline if the salt content gradually gets out of the target range. Check your salinity or specific gravity weekly.

ALKALINITY

When you start keeping stony corals or *Tridacna* clams, you will also want a calcium and alkalinity test kit. Alkalinity is important because it is related to the bioavailability of carbonate and bicarbonate, both needed to build skeletons and hard shells. It is best kept at a range of 2.5 to 4.0 meq/L (milliequivalents/liters) or, if you use the German measure dKH (degrees of Karbonat Haerte, or carbonate hardness), between 7 and 12 (you can convert dKH to meq/L by dividing the dKH number by 2.8). Many inexpensive buffers are available to boost alkalinity.

CALCIUM

Calcium is an essential component in stony coral and clam shell growth. Most reef aquarists attempt to keep their calcium levels at between 400 to 450 ppm Ca^{++}. This can be hard to do if your tank is full of stony corals and may require frequent additions of a calcium supplement such as kalkwasser (limewater) or the use of a calcium reactor on the tank. Fortunately, there are now a number of different two-part balanced additive solutions that allow you to maintain both alkalinity and calcium levels, which is easier to deal with for the more technically challenged and those who prefer not to mess with the dosing of caustic kalkwasser. (For an in-depth look at these subjects see Randy Holmes-Farley's articles at www.advancedaquarist.com.)

pH

Testing the pH of the water from time to time is prudent for either a fish-only or reef tank. Most marine organisms are not very tolerant of rapid changes in the pH (say, over 0.2 points per day) and most do best at a range of 8.0 to 8.4. (Natural seawater has a pH of 8.2.) Also, by maintaining high alkalinity you can prevent precipitous drops in the pH. Marine aquariums tend to become more acidic over time, and a simple pH test will tell you if more water changes or other corrective measures are needed.

NITRATE

Nitrate is not regarded as toxic to fishes, except at very high levels, but reef aquarists like to keep it at a minimum, primarily to prevent blooms of nuisance algae. High nitrate levels have also been associated with corals losing their bright colors and turning tan or brown. Nitrate can be controlled by not overfeeding or overstocking fish, by using a good skimmer or algae filter, by doing regular water changes, and by keeping filter media clean. Try to keep nitrate levels below 5 ppm; serious reef aquarists aim for less than 2 ppm.

PHOSPHATE

Phosphates are natural by-products of aquatic life, but in the aquarium they can be powerful stimulants of algae growth. In addition to phosphates excreted by animals, they enter the aquarium via foods and tap water. Reef aquarists aim to keep their phosphate level at zero, although precise measurements are hard to come by. The best methods for keeping phosphate levels down are not overfeeding or overstocking, efficient protein skimming, growing macroalgae in a lighted sump, running tap water through a reverse osmosis unit, and using phosphate reducing media (Rowaphos, Phosguard, Phosphate Sponge, and others).

Light up your photosynthetic life

Lighting has traditionally been the biggest barrier keeping marine hobbyists from trying their hands at reefkeeping. Fortunately, the cost of providing intense light in the appropriate spectrum has declined dramatically.

The need for bright lighting is driven by the fact that there are a number of popular aquarium invertebrate groups that rely on photosynthesis as a primary or supplemental source of their nutrients.

The gloriously colored fleshy mantle of a Giant Clam (Tridacna gigas) is packed with millions of zooxanthellae, microscopic algal cells that carry on photosynthesis and provide energy both for themselves and for the clam.

These animals have microscopic algae cells living in their tissues. The symbiotic relationship between these plants and their hosts is a form of mutualism—that is, both organisms mutually benefit from the association. The invertebrate provides a growing substrate and shelter for the algae, while the alga produces energy-rich nutrients (sugars) and oxygen as a result of its photosynthetic activities.

These algae, known as zooxanthellae, live in the tissues of certain sponges, corals, clams, sea slugs, jellyfish, and others. They are unicellular algae, most of which belong to a taxonomic group of brown algae known as dinoflagellates. Of course, in order to photosynthesize, the chlorophyll-impregnated algae needs light.

There is often a minimum intensity and a particular spectral quality of light required for these algae to thrive. If these minimum requirements are not met and the plant-partner should perish, the host invertebrate will often die as well. In some cases, when the invertebrate is stressed (e.g., when water temperature rises above an optimal level) it will purge its zooxanthellae. This is what happens when stony corals bleach. Some algae-bearing invertebrates supplement the nutrients provided by their dinoflagellate partners by ingesting food. The food eaten may include plankton (both minute animals and plants), bacteria, and organic sediments and mucus. Some of these invertebrates may live on stubbornly, if their algae should die off—particularly if they are fed.

When it comes to lighting intensity, there are species-depen-

*A Bubble Coral (*Plerogyra sinuosa*) is a large-polyped stony coral that can thrive in moderate lighting, provided it is given meaty foods regularly.*

dent variations, but we can make some generalities when talking about zooxanthellae-hosting corals and clams. Of course, we are all looking for the "cookbook" formula on how many watts, lumens, or how much PAR (photosynthetically active radiation) should be used per gallon of tank. While there are a number of variables involved in how much light will be transmitted into the tank (e.g., water clarity, distance from lamp to the animal, position of animal relative to light source), the benchmarks widely accepted are as follows:

Moderate Light: 3 to 4 watts per gallon
Bright Light: 5 to 8 watts per gallon

There are many variables, but this assumes a tank that is no more than 24 inches deep. Moderate lighting of 3 to 4 watts/gallon would be an acceptable level for some large-polyped stony corals and many soft corals. Bright light of at least 5 watts/gallon would allow the keeping of many stony corals and giant clams. (See the individual species accounts for specific lighting recommendations.)

The lighting systems used on most invertebrate aquariums consist of one or more of the following: standard fluorescents, compact fluorescent lamps (CFL), very high output (VHO) fluorescents, T5 fluorescents, and metal halides. (You may also have heard of HQI

[Halogen Quartz Iodide] lamps—these are compact metal halide bulbs that produce high-intensity light.)

To achieve a ratio of 5 watts/gallon or more is certainly easier with higher output lamps. Let's consider a 75-gallon aquarium that will house small-polyp stony (SPS) corals that require bright light conditions. Let's shoot for 5 watts/gallon—that is, a total of 375 watts of light over the tank. In order to achieve this it would take around 10 standard fluorescent bulbs (40 watt), six power compacts (65 watt), or one or two metal halide lamps.

The T5 fluorescent bulb is now popular on the reef scene. It is a much narrower bulb that puts out more intense light than the standard fluorescent. For our 75-gallon SPS coral aquarium, it would take seven T5 bulbs to exceed our 5 watts per gallon. Conveniently enough, there is a standard fixture on the market that has eight T5 bulbs delivering 432 watts. In order to get enough light over most display aquariums that contain bright-light demanding inverts, it is best to use metal halides or T5 fluorescents. (Nano reefs are more easily lit by power compacts.)

Metal halides are the best choice for tanks deeper than 24 inches, but they have some drawbacks: they produce lots of heat, the bulbs get hot and will explode if water is splashed on them, they produce more harmful UV light (which can damage some corals and clams), and they are also expensive to buy, run, and maintain. It is important to keep some distance between your metal halides and the water's surface (a minimum of 8 inches) and to employ circulation fans to dissipate heat.

Most aquarists elect to purchase prepackaged lighting systems that come complete with the appropriate lamps and fixtures, reflectors (that ensure more light is directed into the tank), a protective splash lens, and cooling fans (to dissipate some of the heat energy the lamps produce). Systems "armed" with metal halides also have acrylic shields that absorb the UV radiation produced by the bulb. Premade lighting systems can be purchased for tanks as small as 2 gallons to tanks as long as 6 feet.

It is not unusual for a more sophisticated lighting system to include LED moon/lunar lights. These bulbs produce about one watt of blue light and remain on when all the other lights are extinguished. This low-power lamp serves to replicate the glowing moon at night. It is thought that this may encourage more normal nighttime activity in your captive reef animals, including spawning, nighttime feeding, and refuging.

Can you have too much light over the tank? As you will see in the species accounts in this book, there are some corals that prefer more moderate light levels. There are also animals that do not use zooxanthellae as a nutrient source that will spend more time in the open in a dimly lit aquarium. In the case of shallow-water corals, it is nearly impossible to put too many light fixtures over tanks and harm them. It is possible to burn shallow-water animals with lamps that produce excessive amounts of UV light. You might also damage corals or clams that have been kept in a poorly illuminated holding aquarium for a long time before arriving in your tank. It is prudent to acclimate corals and clams gradually to high-intensity lighting when first acquired (see the acclimation section below for more on this). Sudden exposure to very bright lighting can prove fatal to sensitive invertebrates.

Corals and clams have pigments that act as a sun block. These pigments also give the coral and clams their amazing colors. If corals and clams are relocated into an aquarium that has a different light source than they are accustomed to, they may change color. In some cases, beautiful corals may change to barnyard brown—a real disappointment if you paid good money for that resplendent colony.

Invertebrate acclimation

Many invertebrates are very sensitive to sudden changes in environmental parameters. For example, soft corals, shrimps, and most echinoderms can be done in by sudden changes in salinity. A soft coral, sea urchin, or starfish that has been shocked may droop, deflate, melt down, or disintegrate over a period of hours or days. A shrimp that has been mishandled may simply keel over dead right before your eyes.

Abrupt parameter shifts are most likely to occur when you move an invert from a supplier's tank to your own. When a live organism is placed in the limited amount of water in a closed plastic bag, changes will occur. Oxygen levels and pH drop and ammonia levels rise. The extent of change depends on transport time. If the animal

Drip acclimation using a length of flexible airline tubing with a loose knot or valve at the lower end allows incoming shipping water to be mixed very slowly with water from the aquarium where the new animals are to be housed.

is shipped from Wisconsin to California, it might be in the shipping bag for 24 hours. As a result there will be more potentially dangerous changes in water parameters than there would be if the same animal had traveled via car from a hometown fish store. But there are also likely to be differences in the water parameters between your local fish store's display tanks and your aquarium. No matter where your invert comes from, slowly acclimating it to a new home is imperative to its health.

The most effective way to make these adjustments is to drip or dribble water from your tank into the transport water where the new invert still rests. Simply take a long piece of flexible silicone airline tubing, start a siphon, and then tie a loose knot near the bottom end of the tubing. Tighten the knot so that water is dripping very slowly from the tube. (A more sophisticated but still inexpensive method is to attach a plastic air valve to the end of the tubing to control the flow rate.) Place the dripping end in the transport bag, or even better, gently pour the bag's contents into a bucket that is *only* used for aquarium tasks. Take a clothespin and clip the airline tubing to the side of the bucket so it does not accidentally fall out and create a flood.

The toughest part of this technique is knowing how much water one should "drip" into the bag/bucket before placing the invert into the aquarium. I have known aquarists to use this method over many hours (in one case six hours), which I believe is excessive. (Keep in mind that you would have to be sure that temperature and dissolved oxygen content did shift appreciably over this period.) I would recommend that you slowly drip water into the transport container holding the new animal so that the water volume increases three to five times in an hour. At this "drip rate," the animal should be ready to be placed in the aquarium in one to two hours. Some aquarists take it one step further—they measure the specific gravity, pH, and temperature of the water in the bucket periodically until they match the tank's water parameters. Then they release the new animal into the aquarium.

Zooxanthellae-bearing invertebrates may also need to be slowly acclimated to a new lighting system. If the animal has been held in relatively low light conditions for some time, you should not place it high in an aquarium with intense lighting (e.g., metal halides). Instead, the organism should be placed near the bottom of the tank, off to the side of the central light core. Over several weeks, it can be moved higher "up the reef" and into a position where it gets the full amount of light required.

You can also use a light shield to protect newly introduced sessile invertebrate. Simply place a piece of UV-shielding acrylic between the invert and the light source. Pull the acrylic away for longer and longer durations until you are ready to remove it completely. If the tissue of a new coral or clam exhibits signs of bleaching, which means that areas lack the pigments that protect them from UV rays, you may want to make the lighting transitions even more slowly.

When moving sponges, mollusks, crustaceans, or echinoderms from the transport container into your aquarium, try not to remove them from the water. It is possible that air could be trapped in the bodies, shells, exoskeletons, or tests of these animals, which could cause health problems.

Remember that all invertebrates must be acclimated slowly. Even seemingly bulletproof animals such as snails can easily be killed or severely weakened by abrupt changes in salinity, pH, and temperature.

Invertebrate foods & feeding

Invertebrates feed in several different ways. Many are heterotrophic—that is, they cannot produce their own food but must ingest organic substances for nutrition. These animals ingest plant material (herbivores), animal prey (carnivores), or both (omnivores). Some inverts (detritivores) also feed on detritus or decomposing organic materials and the associated bacteria/microorganisms.

Many heterotrophic invertebrates feed on plankton—either phyto (plant) and/or zoo (animal). Those species that strain food particles from the water column are known as suspension feeders or filter feeders. Planktivores usually have specialized structures (often associated with the gills) that enable them to trap these food

Small crabs, such as this Xenia crab, and other commensal and parasitic hitchhikers frequently make their way into the aquarium on colonies of wild corals.

items. Many filter-feeding animals also absorb inorganic and organic materials from the water column.

Invertebrates are autotrophic if they derive nutrients from the photosynthesis carried out by the zooxanthellae (algal symbiont cells) that live in their tissues. This is the case with *Tridacna* clams that rely on their zooxanthellae partners to produce most of their nutrients. These animals must get enough light for the algae in their tissues to photosynthesize. If the algae dies, so does the host clam. There are no marine animals that get 100 percent of their nutrients from their algae partners—they are better recognized as mixotrophic; that is, they rely on both autotrophic and heterotrophic feeding strategies.

In order to take care of invertebrates, we need to know what they eat and how they nourish themselves. Fortunately, for modern-day reefkeepers, this information is readily available. There are now a host of foods available to help target the nutritional needs of invertebrates. When selecting a food, look for one that is rich in proteins, amino acids, and HUFAs (highly unsaturated fatty acids). These nutrients are essential for keeping inverts healthy. Some foods are replete with pigments such as beta-carotene and astaxanthin that can help maintain an animal's color.

FOODS FOR FILTER FEEDERS

Suspension feeders ingest tiny food particles. Some animals that feed in this manner can derive enough nutrition from the food particles added for fishes, so their nutritional needs will not need to be specifically targeted. But most suspension feeders ingest very tiny food particles and need to be offered special preparations.

A number of filter-feeding soft and stony corals, sea anemones, feather duster worms, and clams ingest phytoplankton. While these algae cells are very small (around 4 to 20 micrometers in diameter), they are an important food as they tend to be rich in omega-3 fatty acids. Phytoplankton is available in a number of different forms, including liquid, dried, and frozen paste. Although it is the most nutritious and it's hard to overfeed, live phytoplankton is expensive and must be refrigerated.

Another option is algal paste, phytoplankton species in frozen form (e.g., Instant Algae from Reed Mariculture). It is very nutritious,

A well-camoflaged Phyllodesmium *slug grazes on a patch of Green Star Polyps. Some aquarists happily tolerate the presence of such interesting predators.*

easy to store, and less expensive than live food, but since you're adding dead plant material to the tank, water quality will degrade if you overfeed.

Dried phytoplankton is also available (e.g., ESV Spray-dried Marine Plankton). It has good nutritional value and is inexpensive, but the algae in this product is usually too large for many phyto-planktivores. It should be placed in blender prior to feeding for two minutes to decrease particle size, and is best kept refrigerated.

Finally, there are the liquid phytoplankton substitutes, which are typically sold on the shelf at your local aquarium stores. The best of these is Marine Snow (Two Little Fishes). It's easy to store and includes zooplankton and dissolved organics but somewhat expensive and less nutrient-rich than other foods. (For more on this topic, see Dr. Rob Toonen's many articles on the subject on the Internet.) Suspension-feeders that feed mainly on phytoplankton will have to be fed daily as they typically take in nutrients throughout the day (or night) in the wild.

Zooplankton is also an important food to some suspension-feeding inverts, including stony corals, gorgonians, sea fans, sea anemones, worms, zoanthids, clams, certain crustaceans, and echinoderms. There are a number of zooplankton/zooplankton-

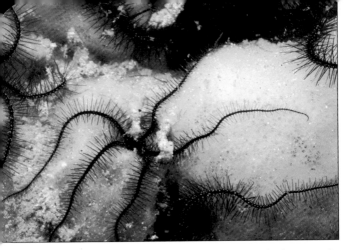

Spiny Brittle Stars (Ophiothrix sp.) are excellent detrivores, cleaning up uneaten food, fish wastes, and other debris that lands on the aquarium substrates.

substitutes on the market. Oyster larvae, salmon roe, rotifers, copepods, and cyclops are often used. Frozen Cyclop-eeze, composed of tiny orange crustaceans in the genus *Cyclops*, is a great new food for zooplanktivores since it has high concentrations of the pigment astaxanthin and HUFAs. There are many dry foods that include phytoplankton. Beware that some of the "zooplankton in a bottle" (zooplankton "slurries") can have a negative impact on water quality if overfed, which is easy to do.

DETRITUS FEEDERS

Those species that feed heavily on detritus may have a head start if they are introduced to an established aquarium that already has a good supply of this material available. There are suspension feeders (e.g., some soft corals) that ingest detritus particles that are stirred up in the water column by the sand-sifting activities of certain gobies.

HERBIVORES

Most herbivores will need a healthy algae crop to graze on if they are to thrive in the home aquarium. It is extremely important not to overstock your tank with herbivores. When the algae is gone, the animals are likely to starve. That said, some herbivore diets can be supplemented with plant-based foods. These include dried algae sheets (Sea Veggies, *Spirulina*, and sushi-wrap nori), frozen herbivore preparations, tablet, wafer, or stick foods that contain algae,

*Many invertebrates, such as this Blue Swimming Crab (*Portunus pelagicus*) feeding on a sea urchin, are voracious predators and require appropriate foods.*

and algae-flake foods. Animals that will benefit from these foods include many mollusks, crustaceans, sea stars, and urchins.

CARNIVORES

Those invertebrates that feed on larger food items can be fed a variety of seafoods (including shavings or chunks of clam, mussel, squid, shrimp, crab, or non-fatty marine fish flesh), frozen mysid shrimp, and krill of various sizes. It is a good idea to thaw frozen foods in a cup of cool water and pour off the juices, as they can impact water quality. Some carnivores will also eat freeze-dried and flake foods. Large polyped stony corals (e.g., *Trachyphyllia*, *Lobophyllia*, *Fungia*) and sea anemones can be fed pieces of sea-food or small, whole marine fish such as silversides that are placed on the fleshy polyp (if they reject it, remove the food promptly).

REFUGIA

A refugium, a body of water that is separate from the main aquarium but shares a common water flow, can be a great source of food for zooplankton feeders. One of the main functions of these remote reservoirs is to provide a breeding sanctuary for various zooplankton and other invertebrates that are likely to be decimated by invertebrates and fishes in the main display tank. These invertebrates may include sponges, bryozoans, snails, sea slugs, worms, shrimp, tiny crustaceans (these are sometimes referred to collectively as "pods"), and brittle stars. When the water flows from the refugium

*The Peacock Mantis Shrimp (*Odontodactylus scyallarus*) is a great aquarium animal, but a notorious predator on other invertebrates and small fishes.*

back into the main aquarium, some of the these zooplankton and/ or invertebrate larvae are available to the animals in the display tank. There are many zooplankton-feeding animals that will do much better in the home aquarium if live food is consistently (or at least more regularly) available to them. A productive refugium can provide this source of natural prey. Healthy live rock aquascaping and an established deep sand bed in the aquarium itself can also be a natural source of small crustaceans, worms, and zooplankton for suspension feeders.

Top 10 invert killers

1. Sudden environmental changes: While invertebrates that live on intertidal reef flats are often exposed to sudden changes in temperature and salinity, many of the animals in our aquariums will suffer—and in some cases such shocks can be lethal. It is important that you regularly check your equipment and that you have a backup power source in case of emergencies. When you do water exchanges, be sure the temperature and salinity of the water to be added is similar to that of the water siphoned out of the tank. Light shock can also be a problem. A coral or clam kept in a dark holding facility for weeks may be damaged or killed if it is suddenly placed under intense lighting. These animals should be allowed to gradually adjust to bright lights.

2. Poor acclimation technique: When you transfer an invert from your local store or if it arrives from a mail-order supplier, it is imperative that it be slowly acclimatized to its new home. See page 28 for tips on invert acclimation techniques.

3. Poor placement: This problem applies mainly to non-motile invertebrates that cannot move to a microhabitat where their needs are better met. This would include most stony corals, soft corals, and clams. If these animals are not placed in a spot in the tank where they get adequate light and water motion, they may not be able to produce enough nutrients or could be suffocated in their own mucus or in detritus. It is similar to landscaping your backyard—there are perennial plants that need more sun, while others prefer shade. If you place them in the wrong microhabitat, they suffer. There is another problem with placement: some corals use chemicals and stinging tentacles to attack encroaching neighbors. If you place one of these aggressive corals too close to another cnidarian or other substrate-attached animal with soft tissue, it is likely to sting or "burn" them and may even lead to their demise. Some corals compete for space by vigorously overgrowing tankmates. Look into the aggressiveness of a species when choosing your livestock.

4. Inadequate lighting: This is a problem especially to inverts that rely on the sun and symbiotic algae as a nutrient source. If these animals are placed under aquarium lighting that is not of the right quality and intensity, they will not grow, and maybe even shrink

Poor water conditions leading to overgrowths of nuisance algae are a major cause of sessile invertebrate deaths. Urchins, however, thrive on lush grazing.

or succumb to disease or starvation.

5. Algae blooms: Sessile invertebrates, like colonial polyps, stony corals, and zoanthids, are sometimes overgrown by pestilent algae. In most cases, these are filamentous green algae or cyanobacteria. If you have macroalgae in your tank, such as *Caulerpa*, it, too, can smother sessile inverts, shielding those animals with zooxanthellae from life-giving light. Boring algae, species that drill into stony coral skeletons and clam valves, are a less common cause of mortality.

6. Improper diet/feeding: As you will see in the species descriptions that follow, inverts feed in many different ways. It is imperative that you know how and what your animals eat. If they rely on zooxanthellae, you must provide adequate light. If they are suspension feeders, you will need to add the appropriate foods. Death by starvation can take months in some invert species. With the much-improved selection of fish and invertebrate foods available, many formerly difficult-to-keep animals can be kept healthy in the aquarium.

7. Parasites: While most are familiar with the names of infamous fish parasites, fewer hobbyists are aware that there are equally virulent invertebrate parasites. Coral parasites (e.g., the infamous "red bugs") can reach epidemic levels and wipe out whole coral communities. For this reason, quarantining inverts for a couple of weeks is a prudent idea. See the care tips for the various invertebrate groups for more details on potential pests and parasites.

8. Copper and other metals: Most inverts cannot tolerate copper. This metal is sometimes employed to treat fish parasites such as ich but should never be added to a tank that contains invertebrates. Placing invertebrates into a tank that has been treated with copper in the past may also cause invert death. Copper molecules can bind to calcium carbonate substrate and may be released into solution if there is a change in pH. If a tank has been "coppered," remove all the carbonate substrate before adding inverts. Some recommend using carbon, a copper-removing filter media, or Poly-Filters to extract copper from a system. Never pour water from a retailer's tank into your own aquarium. If it is a fish-only system the fish is removed from, the water may be treated with copper.

9. Hungry fishes: It should go without saying, but predation happens. Big fish eat little fish and fish of all sizes love to eat invertebrates. Occasionally, even a fish considered reef-safe goes over to "the dark side." For example, there are surgeonfishes and rabbitfishes that are often acquired to help control algae. These fishes sometimes go astray and begin nipping on coral flesh. This often happens if they are not fed enough or if they are exposed to a fish that already has these bad habits. Some invertebrates are more susceptible to fish attack during certain stages of their life cycles. For example, crustaceans are more prone to being eaten by fishes and other crustaceans during or just after molting, when their new armor has not yet hardened. For more in-depth information, see *Reef Aquarium Fishes* (Michael, 2005).

10. Hungry invertebrates: There are some potentially voracious predators among the many invertebrates sold to aquarists. Larger hermit crabs, lobsters, octopuses, and some shrimps will prey heavily on other invertebrate tankmates. Additionally, some invertebrates can exude poisons capable of wiping out a tank. See Invertebrates to Avoid, page 154, for some of the worst offenders.

Field guide to aquarium invertebrates: Species that can thrive for you

For the marine aquarium enthusiast picking out his or her first invertebrate or first coral colony, there is a sense of adventure and the excitement of being able to keep and observe an exotic animal whose origins may have been in remote Tonga, the waters of Hawaii, or a pristine reef in the eastern Caribbean.

However, to be sure that you are not bringing home a bag of woe or an invert that has little chance of a long life in a typical home aquarium, the following 101 species are presented as great choices, especially for less experienced hobbyists.

For intermediate aquarists, there are also some species that require better water conditions, lighting, circulation, and feeding than others. The pleasure of keeping invertebrates is infectious, and that first beautiful cleaner shrimp is likely to be joined by easy-to-keep zoanthids or mushroom polyps. A captive-propagated stony coral colony may not be that far down the road.

For the sake of simplicity, the species are arranged in taxonomic order by phylum (from the most anatomically primitive to most advanced). Within each phylum, animals are further grouped in subtaxa (e.g., order, family). Finally, within these groups, animals are arranged in alphabetical order by common name.

AN INVERTEBRATE-BUYER'S CHECKLIST

I like to encourage aquarists to take their time in selecting a new invertebrate from a dealer's tanks. See an invert you particularly like? Here's a quick checklist of things to ask and watch for before making the decision to buy it.

1. Look for healthy animals. Signs of ill health are taxon specific, but generally avoid specimens that are not alert, that have skin lesions, that are missing appendages, that lack areas of pigment, or that have brown goo covering portions of their tissue.

2. Is the invert eating? If in doubt, ask them to feed the animal and watch to see that it has a healthy interest in food.

3. How long has the dealer had the invert? If it has just arrived, you may want to have them hold it for a few days or a week to be sure it recovers from the stresses of shipping.

CLOVE POLYPS *Clavularia* spp.
(Palm Tree Polyps, Tree Fern Polyps, Glove Polyps)

OVERVIEW: These are encrusting soft corals that spread over rocky substrates and are commendably hardy and easy to keep. Some are exceptionally colorful, but a gamut of color forms makes its way into the aquarium trade, ranging from tan to brilliant white, with shades of green, yellow, and blue. Some are multicolored, with "eyes" and fronds of different hues.

PHYLUM: Cnidaria (Cnidarians).

NATIVE RANGE: Indo-Pacific.

MAXIMUM SIZE: Polyps less than 1 in. (2.5 cm). Colonies may spread over many square yards (meters) in the wild.

MINIMUM AQUARIUM SIZE: 10 gal. (38 L).

LIGHTING: Moderate to bright.

WATER: 75–82°F (24–28°C).

FEEDING: They harbor zooxanthellae and are thus nourished. There is debate on how effective these corals are at exploiting zooplankton and foods for filter feeders.

AQUARIUM COMPATIBILITY: Harmless, but may be impacted by other, more aggressive, corals. Pygmy angelfishes may eat them.

SPECIAL CARE: Needs moderate to strong water currents and room to spread over live rock.

NOTES: Very similar to *Anthelia*. *Anthelia* spp. can deflate, while *Clavularia* spp. fully retract their polyps into rounded closed heads if threatened. *Clavularia* polyps rise from a common, ribbonlike stolon that attaches to rock. Multicolored Clove Polyps, such as those shown above, are highly coveted by reef aquarists.

CLOVE POLYPS *Clavularia* spp.

Larger Clove Polyp species can have tentacles that form a circle of eight tentacles opening to a diameter of almost an inch (2.5 cm). In good conditions, a colony will spread across the substrate and can create new, cloned daughter colonies.

CLOVE POLYPS *Clavularia* spp.

They benefit from wavelike water motion or periodic "washing" with a powerhead or turkey baster to remove any accumulating debris. *Clavularia* polyps arise from a rubbery stolon or mat that clings to the substrate and are hence known as "mat polyps."

GREEN STAR POLYPS *Briareum* spp.
(Star Polyps, Briareum)

OVERVIEW: Arising from a rubbery, reddish mat, these eight-armed polyps will form a beautiful mass of waving arms that is a welcome addition to any aquarium. If provided with good water flow, this highly adaptable species will often flourish and are among the very best soft corals for beginners.

PHYLUM: Cnidaria (Cnidarians).

NATIVE RANGE: Circumtropical.

MAXIMUM SIZE: Colonies may spread to 12 in. (30 cm) in diameter or more. Polyps 0.5 in. (13 mm) tall.

MINIMUM AQUARIUM SIZE: 10 gal. (38 L).

LIGHTING: Moderate to bright.

WATER: 75-82°F (24-28°C).

FEEDING: They harbor zooxanthellae and are thus nourished, but they will ingest some microplankton, especially if tank lighting is not intense.

AQUARIUM COMPATIBILITY: Green Star Polyps seldom encroach on other corals and fit nicely into most reef communities. They may overgrow other sessile inverts. Some shrimps and crabs may attack and nip off the polyps. The nudibranch *Phyllodesmium briareus* preys selectively on them as well.

SPECIAL CARE: Water must be kept low in dissolved nutrients, as various forms of hair and other algae can overgrow and smother colonies of Star Polyps. Direct, strong current may hamper growth.

NOTES: Star Polyps were long known as *Pachyclavularia violacea*. Colors may vary from green to tan and gray.

CABBAGE LEATHER CORAL *Sinularia dura*
(Flower Leather Coral)

OVERVIEW: Although not flamboyantly pigmented, these leafy soft corals are easy to keep and good subjects for beginners venturing into basic reefkeeping. They will tolerate less-than-perfect lighting and water conditions but do best with reef lighting and good water motion. Their leaf-shaped lobes are fringed with polyps that can be extended or retracted.

PHYLUM: Cnidaria (Cnidarians).

NATIVE RANGE: Indo-Pacific.

MAXIMUM SIZE: Colonies to 24 in. (61 cm) in height and width.

MINIMUM AQUARIUM SIZE: 75 gal. (285 L).

LIGHTING: Prefer bright lighting, but can tolerate moderate levels of illumination if they are provided with supplemental foods.

WATER: 75-82°F (24-28°C).

FEEDING: They harbor zooxanthellae and are thus nourished but will benefit from feedings of fine zooplankton several times weekly.

AQUARIUM COMPATIBILITY: Like many soft corals, they can exude toxins to keep other corals from intruding on their territory. Do not place them too close to other coral species.

SPECIAL CARE: All members of the *Sinularia* genus can withstand strong water motion. Direct flow is important to sweep away accumulated debris and mucous.

NOTES: This coral, once established, can easily be propagated by taking cuttings and attaching them to pieces of coral rubble. Healthy colonies reproduce by dropping branches to clone themselves.

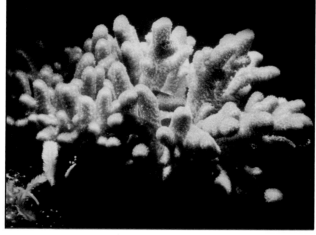

COLT CORAL *Alcyonium* spp.
(Finger Leather Coral, Seaman's Hand Coral)

OVERVIEW: Many aquarists credit Colt Corals with giving them a successful start with their first reef tank. They are hardy, grow well in bright light and with good water movement, and will often multiply rapidly once established. A colony is made up of a mass of fingerlike projections from which polyps of the same color arise.

PHYLUM: Cnidaria (Cnidarians).

NATIVE RANGE: Indo-Pacific.

MAXIMUM SIZE: 6 in. (15 cm) in height.

MINIMUM AQUARIUM SIZE: 30 gal. (114 L).

LIGHTING: Moderate to bright.

WATER: 75–82°F (24–28°C).

FEEDING: They harbor zooxanthellae and are thus nourished but appreciate feedings of phytoplankton and other filter-feeder rations several times weekly.

AQUARIUM COMPATIBILITY: May overgrow other sessile animals. They are rarely bothered by reef-safe fishes and can even be kept with species known to eat stony corals (e.g., butterflyfishes).

SPECIAL CARE: Good aquarium animals. Cuttings from a healthy colony will quickly grow into new colonies and make good barter items among among aquarists.

NOTES: Colors may be white, tan, gray, or yellow. Some 30 species of *Alcyonium* are known, and these and various other genera are sometimes sold as "colt coral." They may easily be confused with *Capnella, Cladiella, Lemnalia,* and *Nephthea.*

COLT CORAL *Cladiella* spp.
(Finger Leather Coral)

OVERVIEW: Here is one of the many soft corals marketed under the name "Colt." They are extremely challenging to identify, even for experts, but are among the easiest soft corals to keep. In good conditions they will grow rapidly and often reproduce. Although not particularly colorful, they sway in the currents and are a pleasing addition to many aquariums. They are not particularly palatable to fishes and may be kept with some species that are not "reef safe."

PHYLUM: Cnidaria (Cnidarians).

NATIVE RANGE: Indo-Pacific.

MAXIMUM SIZE: 16 in. (41 cm) tall.

MINIMUM AQUARIUM SIZE: 75 gal. (285 L).

LIGHTING: Moderate to bright.

WATER: 75–82°F (24–28°C).

FEEDING: They harbor zooxanthellae and are thus nourished but may benefit from feedings of microplankton several times a week.

AQUARIUM COMPATIBILITY: They pose few problems for other invertebrates, although large specimens may shade nearby animals. They are occasionally set back by the presence of too many hermit crabs clambering over their branches. Not bothered by "reef-safe" fishes.

SPECIAL CARE: They respond well to judicious pruning as they get larger, and the aquarist can easily propagate the cuttings into new colonies.

NOTES: Polyps are often a contrasting darker color than the whitish stalks or fingers. Compare to the *Alcyonium* "colt" on page 45.

FINGER LEATHER CORAL *Sinularia* spp.
(Knobby Leather Coral, Flexible Leather Coral)

OVERVIEW: Common and widespread in nature, these corals come in many shapes and colors. Most are leathery to the touch and robust in the aquarium. They will adapt to many different situations but usually do best with bright lighting and vigorous water motion.

PHYLUM: Cnidaria (Cnidarians).

NATIVE RANGE: Indo-Pacific.

MAXIMUM SIZE: 3.3 ft. (1 m).

MINIMUM AQUARIUM SIZE: 75 gal. (285 L).

LIGHTING: Moderate to bright.

WATER: 75–82°F (24–28°C).

FEEDING: They harbor zooxanthellae and are thus nourished but need feedings of microplankton and foods for filter-feeding invertebrates several times weekly if they are to grow.

AQUARIUM COMPATIBILITY: These harmless-appearing animals will actually secret toxins to compete for space in a reef. They may outcompete or even kill other corals. Do not crowd them. Some reef aquarists prefer to keep these corals out of tanks with more delicate stony corals.

SPECIAL CARE: To control their output of toxins and slime, efficient skimming and the use of activated carbon is recommended.

NOTES: Finger Leathers are seen in shades of green, white, yellow, gray, and brown. More than 100 species of *Sinularia* are known. They are easily confused with *Alcyonium* and *Cladiella* species with positive identification requiring microscopic tissue examination.

KENYA TREE CORAL *Capnella imbricata*
(Tree Coral, Cauliflower Soft Coral, Nephthea)

OVERVIEW: Sometimes likened to a weeping willow with gracefully drooping branches, this is a hardy, handsome soft coral that is easily propagated. Colors may be tan, creamy, or brown. A healthy colony will eventually start dropping branches, each of which will become a clone of the parent.

PHYLUM: Cnidaria (Cnidarians).

NATIVE RANGE: Indo-Pacific.

MAXIMUM SIZE: 12 in. (30 cm).

MINIMUM AQUARIUM SIZE: 55 gal. (209 L).

LIGHTING: Moderate to bright.

WATER: 75–82°F (24–28°C).

FEEDING: They harbor zooxanthellae but rely more heavily on feedings of microplankton (including phyto species) and filter-feeder foods to ensure good health. Feed several times a week.

AQUARIUM COMPATIBILITY: They are good aquarium animals, seldom reported to cause issue with other tankmates.

SPECIAL CARE: A well-established colony can be pruned to obtain cuttings that quickly grow into new little "trees." (Affix each cutting to a piece of coral rubble with a rubber band until it attaches itself.)

NOTES: There are 17 species of *Capnella*. They are easily confused with other soft corals. Scottish researchers have isolated three compounds from *Capnella imbricata* that show promise in killing cancer cells associated with certain forms of leukemia and kidney cancer.

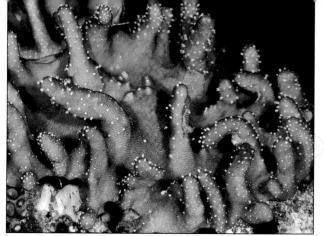

MUMPS CORAL *Lobophytum* spp.
(Lobed Leather, Devil's Hand Coral, Finger Leather)

OVERVIEW: With completely retractable polyps, these leathery, encrusting soft corals can appear lush and fuzzy or rather naked and stark. They are exceptionally hardy, not particularly demanding about light, and easy to keep. A form with ridges rather than finger-like projections is very similar and also hardy in the aquarium.

PHYLUM: Cnidaria (Cnidarians).

NATIVE RANGE: Indo-Pacific.

MAXIMUM SIZE: 3.3 ft. (1 m) in height and width.

MINIMUM AQUARIUM SIZE: 100 gal. (380 L).

LIGHTING: Moderate to bright.

WATER: 75–82°F (24–28°C).

FEEDING: Zooxanthellae provide them with nutrients, but they will also take plankton (both phyto and zoo). Important to feed this coral under suboptimal lighting conditions.

AQUARIUM COMPATIBILITY: May shed toxic films that can land on other corals and cause problems. They have been reported to poison and kill anemones and mushroom polyps. They are rarely nipped by fish tankmates because of toxins.

SPECIAL CARE: Moderate to strong currents, effective protein skimming, and the use of activated carbon will help minimize problems with slime and toxins they may exude.

NOTES: Colors range from green to tan and tones of gray, often with white or light-colored polyps.

RASTA LEATHER CORAL *Sinularia flexibilis*
(Spaghetti Leather Coral, Flexible Leather Coral)

OVERVIEW: These are easily kept corals, occasionally available in beautiful bright green colors, that can grow rampantly in the aquarium. Like other members of their genus, they secrete toxic compounds to establish their territories and deter predation by fishes and other grazers. These toxins can negatively affect other corals and anemones.

PHYLUM: Cnidaria (Cnidarians).

NATIVE RANGE: Indo-Pacific.

MAXIMUM SIZE: 3.3 ft. (1 m).

MINIMUM AQUARIUM SIZE: 100 gal. (380 L).

LIGHTING: Bright.

WATER: 75–82°F (24–28°C).

FEEDING: Zooxanthellae provide them with nutrients, but they will do best with some microplankton feeding.

AQUARIUM COMPATIBILITY: These are aggressive corals that may retard or kill both small-polyp and large-polyp stony corals.

SPECIAL CARE: Moderate to strong currents are needed, along with effective protein skimming and the use of activated carbon to help minimize problems with slime and toxins they may exude.

NOTES: Because of the noxious compounds in their tissue, they are sometimes kept with fishes such as angelfishes and triggerfishes that otherwise would make short work of soft coral polyps. They are easily propagated by slicing off branches and attaching them to pieces of coral rubble to form new colonies.

TREE CORAL *Litophyton* spp.
(Nephthea)

OVERVIEW: These are similar to the Colt and Kenya Tree Corals, but have a stiffer, somewhat spiky appearance. They are hardy, undemanding, and can be quite fast-growing and attain large sizes. Colors vary from a silvery tan to green, creamy, and flesh-colored. They exude toxins and may not coexist well with stony corals.

PHYLUM: Cnidaria (Cnidarians).

NATIVE RANGE: Indo-Pacific.

MAXIMUM SIZE: 3.3 ft. (1 m), larger in the wild.

MINIMUM AQUARIUM SIZE: 75 gal. (285 L).

LIGHTING: Moderate to bright.

WATER: 75–82°F (24–28°C).

FEEDING: Zooxanthellae provide them with nutrients, but they also require microzooplankton feedings several times weekly.

AQUARIUM COMPATIBILITY: They may wage warfare with nearby anemones and stony corals and are not always victorious in these battles. It is a moderately toxic species.

SPECIAL CARE: Moderate to strong currents are needed, along with effective protein skimming and the use of activated carbon to help minimize problems with slime and toxins they may exude.

NOTES: Some aquarists report that *Aiptasia* spp. nuisance anemones will sting and kill *Litophyton* corals. They may reproduce by shedding branchlets that grow into new colonies. The aquarist can also slice off branches from time to time and encourage attachment to pieces of coral rubble.

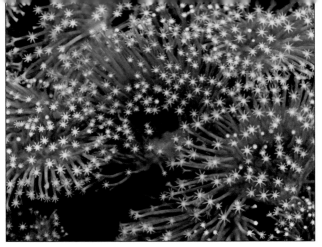

UMBRELLA LEATHER CORAL *Sarcophyton* spp.
(Mushroom Coral, Toadstool Coral)

OVERVIEW: Considered by many to be among the most attractive of all soft corals, these are relatively undemanding animals that sport masses of long, delicate polyps, each tipped with eight tentacles that resemble a starburst. Colors range from tan to green and brilliant yellow. Can live for years and become massive.

PHYLUM: Cnidaria (Cnidarians).

NATIVE RANGE: Indo-Pacific.

MAXIMUM SIZE: 3.3 ft. (1 m) in height.

MINIMUM AQUARIUM SIZE: 100 gal. (380 L).

LIGHTING: Bright.

WATER: 75–82°F (24–28°C).

FEEDING: Zooxanthellae provide them with nutrients, but they will do best in tanks that are fed microplankton and filter-feeding solutions several times weekly. (This is especially true if housed under less-than-optimal lighting.)

AQUARIUM COMPATIBILITY: *Sarcophyton*s possess potent toxins used for defense and for establishing their territory. They may not coexist with stony corals, sea anemones, or mushroom polyps.

SPECIAL CARE: Moderate currents are needed, along with effective protein skimming and the use of activated carbon to help minimize problems with slime and toxins they may exude. They are more sensitive to handling than many other soft corals.

NOTES: Colonies can retract all polyps if conditions are not right, and growing colonies periodically collapse to shed tissue. They usually bounce back, rejuvenated and larger in size.

XENIA CORAL *Xenia* spp.
(Waving Hand Corals, Pulse Corals)

OVERVIEW: Here is great beginner's coral that can mesmerize aquarium viewers transfixed by polyp tentacles that pulse, opening and closing rhythmically as they sway in the currents (this may facilitate feeding). Now widely available as captive-propagated colonies. Colors range from white to creamy, greenish, blue, or silvery.

PHYLUM: Cnidaria (Cnidarians).

NATIVE RANGE: Indo-Pacific.

MAXIMUM SIZE: 4 in. (10 cm) tall.

MINIMUM AQUARIUM SIZE: 10 gal. (38 L).

LIGHTING: Moderate to bright.

WATER: 75–82°F (24–28°C).

FEEDING: Zooxanthellae provide them with nourishment, but they are likely filter feeders and may benefit from the addition of microplankton mixtures.

AQUARIUM COMPATIBILITY: Harmless. May propagate themselves wildly, but most aquarists are pleased to have live rock and tank walls covered in new colonies of *Xenia* spp. They are fed upon by pygmy angels and some specialized sea slugs and crabs. (If polyps disappear, search for a potential culprit hiding in the colony.)

SPECIAL CARE: Do best in moderate, oscillating currents. Avoid rapid shifts in water chemistry that can shock them. May stop pulsing in aquarium for unknown reasons.

NOTES: *Anthelia* spp. corals have polyps that arise from a common encrusting mat, and some do exhibit pulsing behaviors. *Xenia* spp. polyps branch out from a distinctive tree-like stalk.

XENIA CORAL

The pulsing behavior of *Xenia* spp. is suspected to be related to feeding, but this is still unconfirmed by research. Not all colonies will pulse, and they will cease pulsing if water conditions do not suit them. Pulsing behavior is more reliable in captive-bred animals.

XENIA CORAL

Captive-propagated colonies of Xenia tend to fare much better than wild-harvested stock, which may not ship well. Once established, Xenia may spread rampantly on exposed live rock and up onto the walls of the aquarium. It is easily harvested for trade or sale.

CORKY SEA FINGERS *Briareum asbestinum*
(Deadman's Fingers)

OVERVIEW: Gorgonians include many beautiful types of sea fans, sea plumes, and sea rods, most requiring expert aquarium care. This is an exception. It is a species familiar to all snorkelers and divers in South Florida and the Caribbean. It is very hardy and interesting when its polyps emerge to flutter in the currents. The upright branches or fingers are lavender or purple-gray, composed of a horny protein called gorgonin. Polyps are typically brown, sometimes with a green cast.

PHYLUM: Cnidaria (Cnidarians).

NATIVE RANGE: South Florida, Caribbean.

MAXIMUM SIZE: 24 in. (61 cm).

MINIMUM AQUARIUM SIZE: 50 gal. (190 L).

LIGHTING: Moderate to bright.

WATER: 75–82°F (24–28°C).

FEEDING: This species has zooxanthellae, but it will do better if fed small plankton, such as Cyclop-eeze or foods for filter feeders.

AQUARIUM COMPATIBILITY: May grow fast enough to compete with other corals for space. Be sure to give it room to expand.

SPECIAL CARE: Under bright illumination and good water flow it will grow rapidly.

NOTES: In addition to the fingerlike vertical form, this species is also seen encrusting hard substrates with an appearance similar to that of Green Star Polyps (page 43). In good conditions both forms will spread and create new colonies on adjacent pieces of live rock or coral rubble.

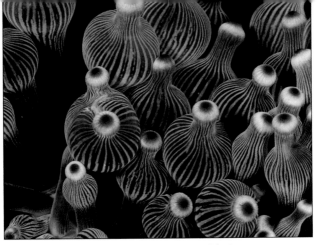

BUBBLE-TIP ANEMONE *Entacmaea quadricolor*
(Bulb-tip, Bulb-tentacle Anemone)

OVERVIEW: Easily the best choice of sea anemones for the aquarist wanting to observe the anemonefish symbiotic relationship. If fed meaty foods regularly, the Bubble-tip Anemone should prove hardy and may even reproduce. Captive-bred specimens are most likely to thrive and are highly recommended.

PHYLUM: Cnidaria (Cnidarians).

NATIVE RANGE: Indo-Pacific.

MAXIMUM SIZE: 12 in. (30 cm) in diameter.

MINIMUM AQUARIUM SIZE: 30 gal. (114 L).

LIGHTING: Bright.

WATER: 75–82°F (24–28°C).

FEEDING: Is partially nourished by its zooxanthellae. Must have regular feedings of meaty foods such as krill, whole or diced shrimp, and marine fish, such as silversides. Some very successful anemone keepers feed daily.

AQUARIUM COMPATIBILITY: May sting nearby corals. May capture and consume aquarium fishes on rare occasions.

SPECIAL CARE: Does best with moderate to strong currents. Needs a rocky substrate where it will bury its attachment disc in a tight niche.

NOTES: Colors vary from brown to bright green. Tentacle tips may be plain or colorful and swell when the animal is thriving. A healthy specimen may split into several (two to five) smaller individuals that may or may not remain together. See the variant Rose Anemone, opposite page.

ROSE ANEMONE *Entacmaea quadricolor*

Seen in many shades of red and pink, this is considered to be a color variety of the Bubble-tip Anemone. It usually commands premium prices, is less common, and is sometimes sold as a separate species, which it is not believed to be.

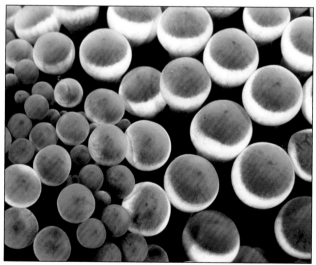

BUBBLE-TIP ANEMONE *Entacmaea quadricolor*

The Bubble-tip Anemone is highly variable in color and is the best choice for aquarists wanting to establish a clownfish-anemone relationship in their aquariums. It is accepted by virtually all species of clownfish and is widely available as a captive-bred organism.

CARIBBEAN GIANT ANEMONE *Condylactis gigantea*
(Haitian Anemone, Condy)

OVERVIEW: This is a hardy species that is a good beginner's anemone. It is highly variable in color, depending on where it was collected and how it is kept. Often seen with a reddish orange column, sometimes tan or green. Tentacle tips may be pink, purple, green, or occasionally yellow. If provided with a rocky aquascape, it will usually sink its column safely into a tight crevice, leaving its tentacles exposed.

PHYLUM: Cnidaria (Cnidarians).

NATIVE RANGE: Tropical Atlantic.

MAXIMUM SIZE: 12 in. (30 cm).

MINIMUM AQUARIUM SIZE: 30 gal. (114 L).

LIGHTING: Moderate to bright.

WATER: 73–84°F (23–29°C).

FEEDING: Is partially nourished by its zooxanthellae. It is a filter feeder, but must have regular feedings of meaty foods such as krill, whole or diced shrimp, and marine fish, such as silversides.

AQUARIUM COMPATIBILITY: It may sting other invertebrates. Most clownfish species will not associate with it, but Clark's Anemonefish (*Amphiprion clarkii*) is an occasional exception. It may serve as a host for anemone shrimps.

SPECIAL CARE: Provide at least moderate currents.

NOTES: The column color can be white or red. The tentacles can be gray or even deep purple. The tentacle tips may swell in the manner of the Bubble-tip Anemone. Plays host to a variety of small crustaceans and fishes.

CURLEYCUE ANEMONE *Bartholomea annulata*
(Ringed Anemone)

OVERVIEW: A familiar sight to snorkelers and divers in South Florida and the Caribbean, this interesting, hardy anemone buries its column in rocky crevices and even in empty conch shells. It is a good beginner's anemone but not likely to serve as a host for clownfishes. Natural symbionts may include cleaner and pistol shrimps.

PHYLUM: Cnidaria (Cnidarians).

NATIVE RANGE: Caribbean.

MAXIMUM SIZE: 8 in. (20 cm) diameter with tentacles extended.

MINIMUM AQUARIUM SIZE: 20 gal. (76 L).

LIGHTING: Moderate to bright.

WATER: 75–82°F (24–28°C).

FEEDING: Carnivore. Must have regular feedings of chopped meaty foods such as krill, whole or diced shrimp, and marine fish, such as silversides.

AQUARIUM COMPATIBILITY: Especially good in a Caribbean biotope tank. Occasionally guilty of catching and eating small fishes. Its long tentacles may be a problem in a crowded reef tank, where it may sting other animals within its reach.

SPECIAL CARE: When it perceives a threat, it will rapidly contract its tentacles.

NOTES: Like all anemones, it may wander around a new aquarium until it finds a suitable spot to settle. During these movements, anemones are vulnerable to damage from powerheads, heaters, and other mechanical devices. It may protectively host commensal crustaceans, including *Alpheus* and *Periclimenes* shrimps.

FLOWER ANEMONE *Epicystis crucifer*
(Rock Flower Anemone, Rock Anemone, Beaded Anemone)

OVERVIEW: These are hardy, attractive, highly variable smaller anemones collected in shallow back reef areas and rubble zones. They have a beaded surface, approximately 200 relatively short tentacles that may be multicolored or beaded. Flower Anemones typically bury most of their body in sand, leaving the tentacles exposed, but may also settle into rocky niches for protection. Colors range from tan to green, purple, white, and mottled.

PHYLUM: Cnidaria (Cnidarians).

NATIVE RANGE: Bahamas, Caribbean.

MAXIMUM SIZE: 5 in. (13 cm) diameter.

MINIMUM AQUARIUM SIZE: 10 gal. (38 L).

LIGHTING: Bright.

WATER: 75–82°F (24–28°C).

FEEDING: Carnivore. Must have regular feedings of chopped meaty foods such as krill, whole or diced shrimp, mussels, and marine fish, such as silversides.

AQUARIUM COMPATIBILITY: Good beginner's reef animal. Will not attract anemonefishes but a favorite of the Anemone Porcelain Crab and some commensal shrimps, including *Periclimenes* spp.

SPECIAL CARE: These anemones make an interesting display in groups with various shades of color. They will readily adapt to a sandy bottom littered with pieces of coral rubble or live rock.

NOTES: *Phymanthus* species anemones from the Indo-Pacific are similar and may also be sold as Sand, Rock, or Flower Anemones. They may have textured or branching tentacles.

HADDON'S CARPET ANEMONE *Stichodactyla haddoni*
(Saddle Anemone, Sand Carpet Anemone)

OVERVIEW: Although not a beginner's anemone, this is widely considered to be the hardiest of the carpet anemones. It can grow large and requires a system with good water circulation, bright light, and efficient skimming or other methods of keeping dissolved organic matter under control. (It is a heavy feeder and creates considerable dissolved waste.)

PHYLUM: Cnidaria (Cnidarians).

NATIVE RANGE: Indo-Pacific.

MAXIMUM SIZE: 31 in. (80 cm) disk diameter.

MINIMUM AQUARIUM SIZE: 100 gal. (380 L).

LIGHTING: Bright.

WATER: 75–82°F (24–28°C).

FEEDING: Is partially nourished by its zooxanthellae but must be fed daily. Offer meaty foods such as krill, shrimp, and marine fish, such as lancefish or silversides.

AQUARIUM COMPATIBILITY: Needs an open, sandy bottom to bury its foot. At least 6 in. (15 cm) of depth is recommended. It will "burn" nearby corals and may eat small aquarium fishes.

SPECIAL CARE: Handle with rubber gloves, as tentacles can be very "sticky." Some aquarists are very sensitive to anemone stings. Acclimate this anemone over a period of hours.

NOTES: Fish species hosted by Haddon's Carpet Anemone include *Amphiprion akindynos, A. chrysopterus, A. clarkii, A. polymnus,* and *A. sebae,* the most common of these being Clark's and the Saddleback Anemonefish.

BULL'S EYE ZOANTHID *Zoanthus* spp.
(Colonial Anemones, Zoanthus Button Polyps)

OVERVIEW: Although devilishly hard to identify with any certainty, the many zooanthid species that make their way into the aquarium trade are virtually all easy to keep if provided reef conditions: bright light, good water motion, and low dissolved nutrient levels.

PHYLUM: Cnidaria (Cnidarians).

NATIVE RANGE: South Florida, Caribbean.

MAXIMUM SIZE: Polyps .5 in. (1.27 cm).

MINIMUM AQUARIUM SIZE: Nano tanks, 2 gal. (8 L).

LIGHTING: Moderate to bright.

WATER: 75–82°F (24–28°C).

FEEDING: Photosynthetic. May ingest some planktonic and filter-feeder foods, but primarily rely on their zooxanthellae.

AQUARIUM COMPATIBILITY: Will spread and battle for space with other corals and sessile invertebrates. Give them room to grow. (They are rather benign and are often killed by more aggressive corals.) Zoanthids may occasionally capture and eat nano-size fish and crustaceans that come to rest on their oral disks.

SPECIAL CARE: All zoanthids have palytoxin in their external mucus and this can cause burnlike rashes, severe allergic reactions, or even more serious health consequences. Treat with respect.

NOTES: The specimens shown on this and the following page were all collected in South Florida. Colors of tropical Atlantic and Caribbean zoanthids range from creamy white to brown, tan, green, and blue, sometimes with contrasting hues and colored "eyes" at the center of their oral disks.

ZOANTHIDS

Seemingly harmless, most zoanthid colonies will spread over a rocky substrate in the aquarium, eventually bringing them into contact with other corals. They win some of these turf battles and lose others. Sea anemones will predictably sting and kill zoanthids.

ZOANTHIDS

Although exceptionally beautiful under Actinic fluorescent light, zoanthids all produce palytoxin that resides in ther mucus and gonads. This is a potent neurotoxin that can seriously affect humans who handle zoanthids without rubber gloves.

GREAT ZOANTHID *Protopalythoa grandis*
(Sun Zoanthid, Giant Zoanthid)

OVERVIEW: Zoanthids are hardy anemone-like soft corals found in all tropical seas. They have stalked polyps that arise from a common base. This Caribbean species can be very attractive, growing slowly in clumps rather than mats, but it can encroach on other corals. All zoanthids have a toxic mucus that aquarists should avoid. (See Special Care, below.)

PHYLUM: Cnidaria (Cnidarians).

NATIVE RANGE: Caribbean.

MAXIMUM SIZE: Polyps up to 2 in. (5 cm) across. 12 in. (30 cm), colony diameter.

MINIMUM AQUARIUM SIZE: Nano tanks, 2 gal. (8 L).

LIGHTING: Bright.

WATER: 75–82°F (24–28°C).

FEEDING: Photosynthetic, but should be fed several times weekly with foods for filter feeders and targeted placement of meaty foods such as mysid shrimp, minced marine fish, or crustacean flesh.

AQUARIUM COMPATIBILITY: Good choice for Caribbean biotopes. If not given room to spread, it may subdue and overgrow neighboring corals.

SPECIAL CARE: This species may burn under direct metal halide. It sheds a waxy film to prevent diatoms from growing on it. Handle with extreme care, using rubber gloves to avoid contact with palytoxin. Treat with respect.

NOTES: Colors vary from white to brown, sometimes tinged with green. Mottled colors are common.

GREEN ZOANTHID *Protopalythoa* spp.
(Button Polyps)

OVERVIEW: Most aquarium zoanthids are collected from shallow, brightly lit areas, and they require strong reef lighting and good currents; otherwise, they are hardy and strong survivors. The many green zoanthids are nearly impossible to identify to species level, but they all make good aquarium animals.

PHYLUM: Cnidaria (Cnidarians).

NATIVE RANGE: Indo-Pacific.

MAXIMUM SIZE: Polyps 1 in. (2.5 cm) in diameter and height. Colonies 12 in. (30 cm) in diameter.

MINIMUM AQUARIUM SIZE: Nano tanks, 2 gal. (8 L).

LIGHTING: Moderate to bright.

WATER: 75–82°F (24–28°C).

FEEDING: Photosynthetic, but should be fed several times weekly with foods for filter feeders and targeted placement of meaty foods such as mysid shrimp, minced marine fish, or crustacean flesh.

AQUARIUM COMPATIBILITY: Must be given room to spread, as its toxic mucus will retard the growth of nearby stony corals and other cnidarians within the zone it treats as its own.

SPECIAL CARE: Avoid placing them where they will be buried by shifting sand. Handle with care using rubber gloves, as they exude palytoxin. (Some Pacific island native tribes are reported to have used palytoxin-tipped spears to paralyze game or human enemies.)

NOTES: The relatively large disc is fringed with a row of tentacles that alternate, projecting up and down. The color is a deep emerald green, often with reddish brown highlights.

SEA MATS *Zoanthus pulchellus, Z. sociatus, Z. coppingeri*
(Green Sea Mats, Polyp Rock)

OVERVIEW: Sometimes called Colonial Anemones, these tightly massed zoanthids make an impressive sight when allowed to blanket a large patch of rocky aquarium substrate. They are easy to keep, grow quickly in good conditions, and come in an endless array of color combinations. (Some aquarists become addicted to collecting as many variations as possible.)

PHYLUM: Cnidaria (Cnidarians).

NATIVE RANGE: Circumtropical.

MAXIMUM SIZE: Polyps to 0.5 in. (13 mm) diameter.

MINIMUM AQUARIUM SIZE: Nano tanks, 2 gal. (8 L).

LIGHTING: Moderate to bright.

WATER: 75–82°F (24–28°C).

FEEDING: Photosynthetic. May ingest some planktonic foods, but mainly rely on zooxanthellae.

AQUARIUM COMPATIBILITY: These are less aggressive than other zoanthids and are more likely to lose turf battles.

SPECIAL CARE: Certain snails, Hingebeak Prawns, and Cleaner Shrimps may prey on these mats. Handle with extreme care using rubber gloves. All zoanthids have palytoxin in their external mucus and this can cause burnlike rashes, severe allergic reactions, or even more serious health consequences.

NOTES: Mat-forming zoanthids are generally acquired on pieces of live rock or coral rubble. Colors vary wildly all shades of green and brown to multihued polyps with orange, blue, red, yellows, purple, and shades of white.

YELLOW POLYPS *"Parazoanthus"* spp.
("Parazoanthus gracilis")

OVERVIEW: Science isn't sure what they are, but these leggy zoanthid polyps have done famously in marine aquariums for decades. They are hardy, sure to multiply in good reef conditions, and add considerable interest with their long tentacles swaying in the currents. The solitary or clustered polyps attach to rock and coral rubble and colors range from bright yellow to light brown, sometimes with shades of green.

PHYLUM: Cnidaria (Cnidarians).

NATIVE RANGE: Indo-Pacific.

MAXIMUM SIZE: 2 in. (5 cm).

MINIMUM AQUARIUM SIZE: Nano tanks, 2 gal. (8 L).

LIGHTING: Bright.

WATER: 75–82°F (24–28°C).

FEEDING: Photosynthetic, but also ingest fish and invertebrate foods added to the tank.

AQUARIUM COMPATIBILITY: Will spread and can be aggressive to other corals and sessile invertebrates. Give them room to grow.

SPECIAL CARE: Reproduces rapidly, and as a result can become a pest, impeding the growth of other sessile inverts. Might produce palytoxin in their external mucus that can cause burnlike rashes.

NOTES: Although aquarium literature usually places this species in the genus *Parazoanthus*, many other confirmed members of this group live in close association with sponges, gorgonians, and other sessile invertebrates and are not photosynthetic. Until it is properly studied, the common name is as good as any.

MUSHROOM POLYPS *Discosoma* spp.
(Mushroom Anemones, Corallimorpharians, Corallimorphs)

OVERVIEW: Sometimes likened to a single coral polyp that lives without a skeleton, these simple animals come in a rainbow of colors and are excellent first cnidarians for the aquarist wanting to experiment with reefkeeping. They will adapt to many different environments, are relatively undemanding, and readily reproduce themselves.

PHYLUM: Cnidaria (Cnidarians).

NATIVE RANGE: Caribbean and Indo-Pacific.

MAXIMUM SIZE: 4 in. (10 cm) diameter.

MINIMUM AQUARIUM SIZE: Nano reefs, 2 gal. (8 L).

LIGHTING: Moderate.

WATER: 75–82°F (24–28°C).

FEEDING: Photosynthetic. They will do best if fed microplankton of various kinds, as well as Cyclop-eeze and newly hatched, enriched brine shrimp.

AQUARIUM COMPATIBILITY: Mushroom polyps, once established, can reproduce rapidly and sometimes become a problem as they may impede growth of other sessile inverts.

SPECIAL CARE: Mushroom polyps typically are placed in the lower third of the aquarium where light levels are never too intense. Some types will do better with brighter light; others seem to thrive in dimmer conditions. Some experimentation may be needed.

NOTES: Identification of the corallimorphs is difficult, even for experts. Smooth-surfaced mushrooms are mostly *Discosoma* spp. Hairy mushrooms are usually members of the genus *Rhodactis*.

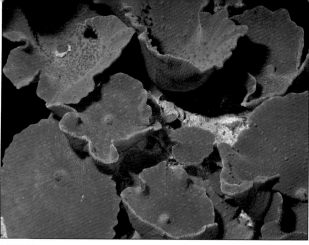

MUSHROOM POLYPS *Discosoma* spp.

Mushroom polyps are sold informally by their colors, which range from solid (above), to metallic, some with multicolored striping or contrasting blotches of pigment. If displayed under strong actinic fluorescent lighting, many have startling fluorescing characteristics.

TONGA BLUE MUSHROOM POLYPS *Rhodactis inchoata*

Members of the *Rhodactis* genus have a fuzzy or warty disc surface covered with short tentacles. Their care requirements are identical to those of *Discosoma* spp. This tentative species is seen in shades of blue and purple and is sometimes sold as Bull's Eye Mushrooms.

MUSHROOM POLYPS *Discosoma* spp.
Known as "corallimorpharians" or corallimorphs, the many types of mushroom polyps are usually sold by their color, rather than species. Older references placed them in the genus *Actinodiscus*, now usually replaced by *Discosoma*.

MUSHROOM POLYPS *Discosoma* spp.
Striped metallic mushrooms are visually striking and highly prized by aquarists. If kept in good conditions, most mushrooms will reproduce by asexual fission, spreading across the rocky substrate of the aquarium and sometimes covering large areas of the bottom.

RICORDEA *Ricordea florida*
(Ricordea, Ricordea Anemone, Florida Corallimorph)

OVERVIEW: Some hobbyists find themselves addicted to collecting every possible color morph of *Ricordea*, a great challenge as new forms constantly seem to turn up in the aquarium trade. These are hardy animals, even for beginners, and they elicit many a "Wow!" from aquarium visitors. Many are now captive-propagated. Colors range from electric green to blue, aquamarine, neon orange, red, yellow, and with some specimens displaying a seemingly impossible mixture of colors on their verrucae (bumps).

PHYLUM: Cnidaria (Cnidarians).

NATIVE RANGE: Circumtropical.

MAXIMUM SIZE: 2.5 in. (6 cm).

MINIMUM AQUARIUM SIZE: Nano tanks, 1 gal. (3.8 L) or more.

LIGHTING: Moderate.

WATER: 75–82°F (24–28°C).

FEEDING: Photosynthetic, but will take microplankton of various sorts, including Cyclop-eeze.

AQUARIUM COMPATIBILITY: Not overly aggressive but may sting encroaching corals that get too close. Good with most reef-safe fishes. May be damaged by pygmy angels, large crabs, and sea slugs.

SPECIAL CARE: *Ricordea* polyps can be placed in brighter illumination to highlight their colors, but not too close to direct metal halide.

NOTES: *Ricordea florida* is found in South Florida, the Bahamas, and the Caribbean. A similar species found across the Indo-Pacific, *Ricordea yuma,* has a highly variable color palette: purple, shades of green, orange, multicolored, and sometimes striped.

ACROPORA *Acropora* spp.
(Staghorn, Bottlebrush, Tabletop Coral)

OVERVIEW: Until the 1990s, coral scientists believed that stony or reef-building corals could never be kept alive in aquariums. Today, dozens and dozens of species of *Acropora* are being propagated and are thriving in home saltwater systems. Aquacultured or "AC" *Acroporas* make excellent starter corals for hobbyists ready to try their hands at these beautiful and varied species.

PHYLUM: Cnidaria (Cnidarians).

NATIVE RANGE: Indo-Pacific.

MAXIMUM SIZE: Up to 10 ft. (3 m) long; most smaller.

MINIMUM AQUARIUM SIZE: 75 gal. (285 L).

LIGHTING: Bright lighting is a must.

WATER: 75–82°F (24–28°C).

FEEDING: These corals gain substantial nutrition from their zooxanthellae, but do better with regular feedings of microzooplankton.

AQUARIUM COMPATIBILITY: Some fishes, slugs, snails, and crabs will eat the polyps. They may shade neighboring corals, but more often come out on the losing end of turf wars with other cnidarians.

SPECIAL CARE: Can be kept in smaller tanks but may quickly outgrow them unless kept trimmed. Cuttings (frags) can be used to start daughter colonies. Wait until a tank is at least a year old before adding an Acropora coral. Acroporids must be provided strong currents and excellent water conditions with high levels of calcium and proper alkalinity. Drastic fluctuations in water parameters are often deadly.

NOTES: The easiest *Acropora* species to keep are branching staghorn types such as the brilliant green *A. yongei* (the "Bali slimer").

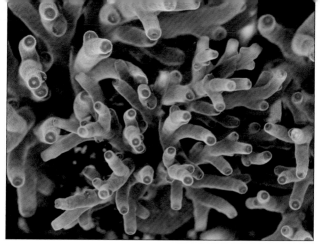

BOTTLEBRUSH ACROPORA *Acropora* spp.

Captive-propagated colonies are much more likely to survive and grow, especially for aquarists with relatively little experience in keeping stony corals. Wild-harvest colonies are much harder to acclimate and should be reserved for experts only.

BALI GREEN ACROPORA *Acropora yongei*, others

This is a great beginner's *Acropora*, exceptionally beautiful, fast-growing, and widely available as "frags" or started colonies, captive-propagated and a proven hardy coral in home aquarium conditions. Many other captive-propagated staghorn types are available as well.

AUSTRALIAN LORD *Acanthastrea lordhowensis*
(Aussie Lord Coral, Acan, Lord)

OVERVIEW: One of the most coveted of stony corals and sometimes fetching astronomical prices for wild colonies, this is actually an easy-to-keep, fast-growing large-polyp stony coral and one of the most beautiful available to aquarists. New colonies will grow from fragments, which lowers the cost of acquisition.

PHYLUM: Cnidaria (Cnidarians).

NATIVE RANGE: Indo-Pacific.

MAXIMUM SIZE: .6 in. (15 cm) for individual polyps. Colonies can be massive.

MINIMUM AQUARIUM SIZE: 20 gal. (76 L).

LIGHTING: Moderate to bright.

WATER: 75–82°F (24–28°C).

FEEDING: Although they possess zooxanthellae, these large-polyped corals are heavy feeders. Offer minced silversides or table shrimp, mysid shrimp, or zooplankton foods for filter feeders every few days. If they are reluctant to feed, try feeding after the lights are off.

AQUARIUM COMPATIBILITY: May eat small, bottom-dwelling fishes such as gobies and pipefishes at night. It will sting and kill other corals that are placed too close. A 6-in. clear zone may be enough.

SPECIAL CARE: Some specimens do better in bright light, others in less-intense situations. Some experimentation may be necessary. Usually do best on the bottom, away from strong direct currents.

NOTES: The three color morphs shown are, clockwise from above: Burning Wild Aussie Lord, Snake Eye Aussie Lord, and Jester Aussie Lord from Vivid Aquariums, Los Angeles. (See Credits, page 191.)

AUSTRALIAN LORD *Acanthastrea lordhowensis*
Propagation of these fleshy large-polyped corals is less difficult than one might imagine. Individual corallites are cut from a healthy colony with a Dremel Rotary Tool saw or poultry shears. Regeneration and recovery is reported to be predictable and quick.

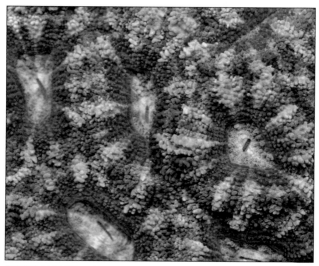

AUSTRALIAN LORD *Acanthastrea lordhowensis*
Color morphs of this coral are many and often astonishing, explaining the elevation of "the Lord" to near cult status with many reef-keepers. Captive-farmed specimens are shown here. They will reach out and sting too-close neighbors if crowded in the aquarium.

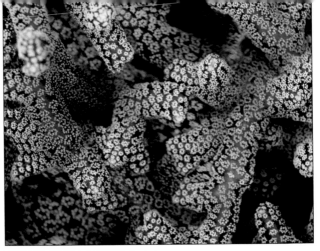

BIRD'S NEST CORAL *Seriatopora* spp.
(Brush Coral)

OVERVIEW: This fast-growing, interesting, and often beautiful coral is widely available as a captive-propagated colony and is much easier to acclimate and keep than those imported from the wild. The thin, brittle branches form compact thickets. In good conditions, branches can be snapped off and will rapidly develop into new daughter colonies.

PHYLUM: Cnidaria (Cnidarians).

NATIVE RANGE: Indo-Pacific, Red Sea.

MAXIMUM SIZE: 12 in. (30 cm).

MINIMUM AQUARIUM SIZE: 55 gal. (209 L).

LIGHTING: Bright light will help maintain the best coloration.

WATER: 75–82°F (24–28°C).

FEEDING: They harbor zooxanthellae but will benefit from feedings of microplankton several times a week.

AQUARIUM COMPATIBILITY: Short sweeper tentacles are employed against more benign relatives, but they are more often damaged by more aggressive cnidarians. Occasionally predatory, polyp-eating crabs will come in with a colony of *Seriatopora*. If patches of missing polyps are seen near a crab, you may want to remove the villian.

SPECIAL CARE: A tank should be at least one year old before introducing a *Seriatopora* spp. Strong water flow is required. Colony shape and color are affected by both prevailing currents and lighting. Sudden changes in water parameters can be lethal.

NOTES: The appearance of this species is variable, with branches and polyps having contrasting colors.

PINK BIRD'S NEST CORAL *Seriatopora hystrix*
Also known as Needle Coral, this is a commonly aquacultured species that is often seen in shades of tan to green, yellow, orange, and shocking pink. Bright light and good water are needed to bring out and maintain the brightest coloration. *Seriatopora* colonies are not tolerant of poor water quality.

PINK BIRD'S NEST CORAL *Seriatopora hystrix*
A large wild colony demonstrates the growth potential within small fragments. Branches are brittle and often broken in transit; each may be cultured into a new bird's nest with care. Numerous tiny commensal crabs are commonly found hidden in such colonies.

BRAIN CORAL *Favites* spp.
(Closed Brain Coral, Pineapple Coral, Moon Coral, Maze Coral)

OVERVIEW: There is a mystique surrounding brain corals, especially these so-called "closed brain corals," but they are actually hardy and undemanding compared with many other stony coral types.

PHYLUM: Cnidaria (Cnidarians).

NATIVE RANGE: Circumtropical.

MAXIMUM SIZE: Potentially massive in the wild.

MINIMUM AQUARIUM SIZE: 100 gal. (380 L) or more.

LIGHTING: Moderate to bright.

WATER: 75–82°F (24–28°C).

FEEDING: Brain corals gain nourishment from their symbiotic zooxanthellae, but they should be fed to encourage growth. They will grasp and consume mysid shrimp as well as minced table shrimp and marine fish, such as silversides. Most of this feeding naturally occurs at night, so nocturnal target feeding is beneficial.

AQUARIUM COMPATIBILITY: Exceptionally good reef-tank corals, but some species have potent, stinging sweeper tentacles that they will extend if placed too close to other corals.

SPECIAL CARE: Be sure to give any brain coral plenty of room to grow. Best placed on hard surfaces, as sand can cause tissue irritation. Moderate to strong water flow is best.

NOTES: *Favites* spp. are often confused with other brain-type corals, especially *Favia*. In this genus, the corallites are separated by a common wall. In *Favia*, each corallite has its own surrounding ridge of skeleton (see pages 90–91). These animals appear much different at night, when their feeding tentacles are unfurled.

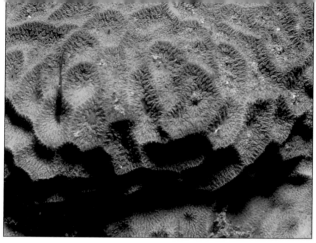

BRAIN CORAL *Favites* spp.

Note the continuous ridge of skeleton that divides the individual large coral polyps. Compare to *Favia* (pages 90–91) and *Platygyra* (page 87), which have somewhat similar appearances. *Favites* corals can slowly reach impressive sizes in aquaria.

BRAIN CORAL *Favites* spp.

Brain corals such as this appear benign but will extend long sweeper tentacles at night if they detect, through chemical sensing, the nearby presence of potential competitor corals. Provide an open or neutral zone of at least 6 inches around such specimens.

BUBBLE CORAL *Plerogyra sinuosa*
(Grape Coral, Octobubble Coral)

OVERVIEW: Although they may appear delicate, these attention-grabbing corals are quite resilient. The vesicles or bubbles that inflate from the polyps expose their zooxanthellae to sunlight. At night they change appearance, with numerous feeder tentacles extended to capture passing zooplankton.

PHYLUM: Cnidaria (Cnidarians).

NATIVE RANGE: Indo-Pacific.

MAXIMUM SIZE: 12 in. (30 cm) diameter or more for colonies.

MINIMUM AQUARIUM SIZE: 75 gal. (285 L).

LIGHTING: Will adapt to various levels of light, from dim to bright. Do not suddenly expose a colony to intense lighting, as it may be shocked and bleached.

WATER: 75–82°F (24–28°C).

FEEDING: Must be fed meaty foods at least several times weekly. Mysid shrimp, chopped marine fish, or crustacean flesh targeted to the colony after dark will be taken greedily.

AQUARIUM COMPATIBILITY: A classic reef aquarium species, but it can attack nearby corals with long, potent sweeper tentacles. Do not place in a crowded location. Polyps rarely nipped by herbivorous fishes sometimes harass LPS corals (e.g., tangs).

SPECIAL CARE: Handle with care and place securely in the reef. Rough handling can trigger fatal infections. Some water movement needed to wash away debris, but no strong, direct current.

NOTES: Bubble Corals in the aquarium trade range from pearly white to various shades of tan, green, and blue, sometimes striped.

CACTUS CORAL *Pavona cactus*
(Potato Chip Coral, Lettuce Coral)

OVERVIEW: The various members of the *Pavona* genus tend to be relatively forgiving of less-than-perfect conditions and a good choice for beginners. Shapes of these corals tend to be highly "plastic," in the words of coral biologists, meaning they can assume many forms in different locales and environmental conditions. Huge beds of this coral are common in the wild.

PHYLUM: Cnidaria (Cnidarians).

NATIVE RANGE: Indo-Pacific, Red Sea.

MAXIMUM SIZE: 33 ft. (10 m) in wild colonies.

MINIMUM AQUARIUM SIZE: 75 gal. (285 L).

LIGHTING: Moderate to bright.

WATER: 75–82°F (24–28°C).

FEEDING: Symbiotic algae provide much of their nutrient needs. Offer fine good particles after the lights are dimmed. Reef plankton, mysid shrimp, reef "snow," and other coral rations can be directed to the colony when its small polyps have emerged.

AQUARIUM COMPATIBILITY: This benign species is often "bullied" by aggressive stony corals and sea anemones and sometimes smothered by fast-growing encrusting cnidarians. May succumb to the chemical warfare than can occur with highly toxic soft corals.

SPECIAL CARE: Individual "leaves" of this coral are easily broken off and each will form a new daughter colony if attached to a piece of coral rubble. Pruning will be required if placed in a small tank.

NOTES: Predominant colors are tan and green, with a fluorescing green sheen in some healthy colonies.

CANDY CANE CORAL *Caulastrea furcata*
(Bull's Eye or Cat's Eye Coral, Torch Coral, Trumpet Coral)

OVERVIEW: These are appealing corals that do well in the hands of reefkeepers of all skill levels. They actually tend to fare better without intense reef lighting or excessively strong circulation. Colors are highly variable, including many shades of tan, brown, and green.

PHYLUM: Cnidaria (Cnidarians).

NATIVE RANGE: Indo-Pacific.

MAXIMUM SIZE: 12 in. (30 cm) tall and wide for colonies.

MINIMUM AQUARIUM SIZE: 75 gal. (285 L).

LIGHTING: Moderate.

WATER: 75–82°F (24–28°C).

FEEDING: Although they possess zooxanthellae, these large-polyped corals are heavy feeders. Offer minced silversides or table shrimp, mysid shrimp, or zooplankton foods for filter feeders every few days. Stop water motion during feeding to allow the polyps to catch and ingest food items that land on their upper surfaces.

AQUARIUM COMPATIBILITY: These are good aquarium animals but will extend stinging sweeper tentacles several inches long if they perceive a competitor is within their territory.

SPECIAL CARE: Moderate, surging current will help keep these corals thriving and free of detritus. Direct, strong lighting from metal halide bulbs may damage this coral.

NOTES: Daughter colonies are easily produced by separating branches from a robust mother colony. With good water conditions, appropriate calcium and alkalinity levels, and regular feeding, this coral can be fast-growing and a source of many new colonies.

CAT'S EYE CORAL *Cynarina lacrymalis*
(Button Coral, Owl Eye Coral)

OVERVIEW: This is a show-stopper coral, an inflatable single polyp that may be larger than a dinner plate, with vibrant shades of red, green, and other colors. A whole silverside placed on its outer perimeter will be maneuvered deftly to the mouth and engulfed. If handled properly and well fed, this beautiful coral grows and flourishes.

PHYLUM: Cnidaria (Cnidarians).

NATIVE RANGE: Indo-Pacific.

MAXIMUM SIZE: 14 in. (35 cm) diameter.

MINIMUM AQUARIUM SIZE: 75 gal. (285 L).

LIGHTING: Moderate.

WATER: 75–82°F (24–28°C).

FEEDING: This coral has zooxanthellae but must be fed. Offer lance-fish, silversides, pieces of marine fish flesh, or table shrimp several times weekly.

AQUARIUM COMPATIBILITY: This coral is reported to be sensitive to the chemicals exuded by mushroom anemones and other soft corals and may not do well in the same system as anemones. *Aiptasia* anemones can kill it. Its fleshy polyp is a tempting target for normally well-behaved pygmy angels, tangs, and rabbitfishes.

SPECIAL CARE: Usually found resting on flat bottom substrates or attached to vertical walls. Do not place directly under intense light or expose it to constant direct currents.

NOTES: The similar *Scolymia* (Doughnut Coral) species do not have a translucent, water-filled, lobed mantle as seen in this species. It is proficient at shedding sand and detritus.

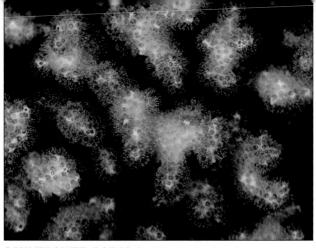

CAULIFLOWER CORAL *Pocillopora damicornis*
(Brush Coral, Cluster Coral, Bird's Nest Coral)

OVERVIEW: This is known among marine biologists as the lab mouse or guinea pig of the coral laboratory, a species long valued for its ease of culture in the aquarium. Captive-propagated colonies are by far the best choice, as domestication tends to result in corals that are much more likely to adapt to different aquarium conditions, settle in quickly, and thrive.

PHYLUM: Cnidaria (Cnidarians).

NATIVE RANGE: Indo-Pacific.

MAXIMUM SIZE: 10 ft. (3 m) in wild colonies.

MINIMUM AQUARIUM SIZE: 100 gal. (380 L).

LIGHTING: Bright light is needed to keep coral from turning brown.

WATER: 75–82°F (24–28°C).

FEEDING: They harbor zooxanthellae but will benefit from feedings of microplankton several times a week.

AQUARIUM COMPATIBILITY: This coral can be somewhat aggressive in paving a way for expansion. It will send out relatively short stinging sweeper tentacles—in the 1 in. (2.5 cm) range—unlike certain other corals that can reach out 10 in. (25 cm) or more.

SPECIAL CARE: Allow room for growth. Strong water movement is a must for this coral to thrive. This species can be more demanding than some other small-polyped stony (SPS) corals.

NOTES: Common colors are green, brown, and pink. Branches can be fingerlike or stubby and not unlike a head of cauliflower. Wild colonies, and even captive-grown specimens, may have commensal or parasitic crabs and other animals hiding in the branches.

HEDGEHOG CORAL *Echinophyllia* spp.

OVERVIEW: The reef aquarium world has been slow to discover the beauties of this genus of plating and encrusting corals, perhaps because they hug hard substrates and often appear as brown, lumpy specimens sometimes likened to elephant hide. Exceptionally easy to keep, *Echinophyllia* is gaining new respect as strikingly beautiful color morphs are found and propagated. Hard to identify and easy to confuse with *Echinopora*, *Oxypora*, and *Mycedium* corals.

PHYLUM: Cnidaria (Cnidarians).

NATIVE RANGE: Indo-Pacific.

MAXIMUM SIZE: Up to 6 ft. (2 m) or more in wild.

MINIMUM AQUARIUM SIZE: 100 gal. (380 L).

LIGHTING: Moderate. In a brightly lit tank, it can be placed in the bottom half of the system.

WATER: 75–82°F (24–28°C).

FEEDING: This coral has zooxanthellae but must be fed pieces of marine fish flesh, table shrimp, or squid once or twice weekly. Will benefit from a regimen of adding various plankton and filter-feeder rations to the aquarium.

AQUARIUM COMPATIBILITY: Peaceful. Give it room to grow and do not place too close to anemones or aggressive corals that are likely to extend stinging sweeper tentacles.

SPECIAL CARE: Does best in low to moderate currents. Do not place directly under intense light at the top of a tank.

NOTES: The coral shown above is a color morph of an unidentified species called "Original Vivid Echinophyllia" by its propagators, Vivid Aquariums in Los Angeles. (See Credits, page 191.)

LOBED BRAIN CORAL *Lobophyllia hemprichii*
(Open Brain Coral, Meat Coral)

OVERVIEW: Most reef aquarists love the many species of *Lobophyllia* for their hardiness, adaptability, and the impressive presence they bring to an aquarium. They are heavy, fleshy corals that respond well to regular feeding of meaty marine foods.

PHYLUM: Cnidaria (Cnidarians).

NATIVE RANGE: Indo-Pacific.

MAXIMUM SIZE: More than 16 ft. (5 m) in diameter in the wild.

MINIMUM AQUARIUM SIZE: 75 gal. (285 L).

LIGHTING: Will adapt to moderate light, but brighter is better.

WATER: 75–82°F (24–28°C).

FEEDING: They are partially nourished by their zooxanthellae, but the feeding tentacles that emerge nightly will greedily take pieces of marine fish, shrimp, squid, and other high-protein saltwater fare. If food is in short supply, the tissue may recede from the edges.

AQUARIUM COMPATIBILITY: *Lobophyllia* spp., with their big polyps, are vulnerable to being stung by other corals. Give them a safe perimeter of space—at least 6 in. (15 cm)—and stop any aggression if it starts to occur. (Use a flashlight at night during feeding time.)

SPECIAL CARE: These corals are tolerant of less-than-perfect conditions and will do best with a stable setting in low or moderate currents. Be sure to keep calcium levels up (400–450 mg/L) to support skeletal growth. Provide moderate water movement.

NOTES: Colors are extremely variable, ranging from drab brown to multicolored polyps with contrast red, powdery gray, violet, green, bronze, and others.

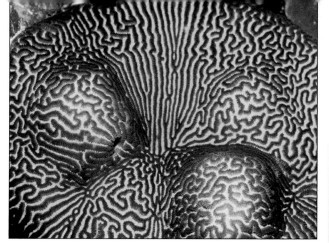

MAZE CORAL *Platygyra* spp.
(Brain Coral, Closed Brain Coral, Worm Coral)

OVERVIEW: These are exotic-looking corals with seemingly infinite maze patterns that delight puzzle lovers and those fascinated by nature's graphic designs. They may be flat or domed and massive in the wild. They usually do well in a basic reef-type aquarium.

PHYLUM Cnidaria (Cnidarians).

NATIVE RANGE: Indo-Pacific.

MAXIMUM SIZE: Several yards (meters) tall and in diameter in the wild.

MINIMUM AQUARIUM SIZE: 100 gal. (380 L).

LIGHTING: Moderate to bright.

WATER: 75–82°F (24–28°C).

FEEDING: *Platygyra* corals are photosynthetic but will benefit from regular feedings of meaty foods, especially at night when their tentacles are extended. Offer zooplankton, mysid shrimp, enriched brine shrimp, and minced marine fish or table shrimp.

AQUARIUM COMPATIBILITY: These are very good reef corals, but they will defend their territory by extending long sweeper tentacles to discourage encroaching cnidarian tankmates.

SPECIAL CARE: If aquarium currents are not sufficient to keep this coral free of debris, use a handheld powerhead or turkey baster to flush away any accumulating detritus.

NOTES: *Oulophyllia* spp. are somewhat similar but have much wider valleys between the skeletal ridges. In the Caribbean, *Diploria* spp. have a strong resemblance to this Indo-Pacific genus.

MONTIPORA *Montipora* spp. (*Montipora confusa*, above)
(Finger Coral, Velvet Coral, many others)

OVERVIEW: One of the most species-rich of the reef-building corals, the genus *Montipora* offers many choices that can make excellent starter species for the aquarium keeper ready to try his or her hand at small-polyp stony corals. Colors can be spectacular, growth is often rapid, and care requirements are not difficult. Shapes vary from branching to plating and whorling, column-forming, and encrusting corals.

PHYLUM: Cnidaria (Cnidarians).

NATIVE RANGE: Circumtropical.

MAXIMUM SIZE: Some are massive in the wild.

MINIMUM AQUARIUM SIZE: 100 gal. (380 L).

LIGHTING: Bright. Some will survive in moderate light conditions but may lose their color.

WATER: 75–82°F (24–28°C).

FEEDING: *Montipora* corals are photosynthetic and most have rather small polyps. They will do better if microplankton and foods for filter feeders are offered to the tank several times weekly.

AQUARIUM COMPATIBILITY: These are not normally aggressive corals, but are often the losers in warfare with other species. Be sure they are given space away from known problem species.

SPECIAL CARE: Plating growth forms are vulnerable to damage from sediment accumulation; appropriate water flow will prevent this.

NOTES: Shape of the colony will be significantly determined by the currents, and much variety may be generated in a single aquarium—even within a single colony.

PLATE MONTIPORA *Montipora capricornis*

Montipora capricornis, above, is beautiful and available as captive-grown colonies or more economical small frags. With good currents, bright light, and plenty of available calcium, this species can show astonishingly fast growth. Finger Montipora corals are also a great beginner's stony coral, available in green or purple.

ENCRUSTING MONTIPORA

Encrusting or mounding Montiporas can be extremely beautiful and tend to be quite hardy and undemanding. They sometimes arrive on live rock and many types are available as starter fragments. Good water conditions and bright light will promote better coloration.

MOON CORAL *Favia* spp.
(Closed Brain Coral, Pineapple Coral)

OVERVIEW: Exotic in appearance and a wonderful addition to any reef aquarium, the many species of *Favia* or Moon Corals are hardy and can be fast-growing. A colony should be provided room to grow with separation from other corals, which it will sting with nocturnal sweeping tentacles if they are too close.

PHYLUM: Cnidaria (Cnidarians).

NATIVE RANGE: Circumtropical.

MAXIMUM SIZE: Some species are massive in the wild.

MINIMUM AQUARIUM SIZE: 100 gal. (380 L).

LIGHTING: Moderate to bright.

WATER: 75–82°F (24–28°C).

FEEDING: *Favia* corals are photosynthetic but will benefit from regular feedings of meaty foods. Offer mysid shrimp, enriched brine shrimp, and minced marine fish or table shrimp.

AQUARIUM COMPATIBILITY: These are good reef animals but cannot be crowded with other cnidarians (corals, anemones, mushroom polyps) or battles will eventually break out.

SPECIAL CARE: Provide a spot on the bottom or rocky shelf in the mid to lower reaches of the tank and keep out of vigorous currents. Do not place too close to sand bed as sand deposits can cause tissue damage.

NOTES: These corals change dramatically when the lights go off. Using a small flashlight, you will see them fuzzy with feeding tentacles and perhaps sweeping their perimeter with long, stinging tentacles to engage too-close competitors. This is the time to feed.

MOON CORAL *Favia* spp.

Corals within this genus vary greatly in color, although glowing shades of green are most common. Other colors seen include cream, yellow, orange, and brown, with many contrasting combinations. Feeding tentacles emerge nightly after the lights dim.

MOON CORAL *Favia* spp.

Favia corallites have their own walls and distinct valleys between polyps. Compare to *Favites*, pages 78–79. Identifying *Favia* species requires examination of the skeleton and considerable expertise. Care requirements are simple and *Favia* can be very long-lived.

OPEN BRAIN CORAL *Trachyphyllia geoffroyi*
(Folded Brain Coral, Crater Coral)

OVERVIEW: These are big, fleshy corals that glow under actinic fluorescent lighting, and strike some viewers as extraterrestrial. They are fascinating and relatively hardy in the hands of aquarists with some reefkeeping experience.

PHYLUM: Cnidaria (Cnidarians).

NATIVE RANGE: Indo-Pacific.

MAXIMUM SIZE: 8 in. (20 cm).

NATIVE RANGE: Indo-Pacific.

MINIMUM AQUARIUM SIZE: 50 gal. (190 L).

LIGHTING: Moderate to bright.

WATER: 75–82°F (24–28°C).

FEEDING: Open brain corals are photosynthetic but will benefit from regular feedings of meaty foods at night when the feeding tentacles are extended. Offer minced marine fish or table shrimp.

AQUARIUM COMPATIBILITY: Keep away from aggressive corals that may attack it with sweeper tentacles. This coral may capture small fishes that perch on its surface. May retract and lose strength if harassed by hermit crabs or fishes that nip at its flesh.

SPECIAL CARE: Place it on the sandy bottom. Will inflate to get rid of any sand that falls on it. A moderate current will facilitate sediment shedding. Directed current can tear the fleshy polyp. Avoid specimens where tissue has receded from skeleton or areas of dead tissue.

NOTES: Colors are highly variable, and multicolored morphs are common. Shades of green and rusty red to pink are most common.

PINEAPPLE CORAL *Blastomussa wellsi*
(Swollen Red Brain Coral)

OVERVIEW: This is a handsome, very durable coral that does best away from intense light. Corallites arise out of individual stony tubes that are joined at the base, but when the mantles are inflated during daylight the colony appears to be a continuous field of connected polyps.

PHYLUM: Cnidaria (Cnidarians).

NATIVE RANGE: Indo-Pacific.

MAXIMUM SIZE: Colonies to 18 in. (46 cm) in diameter.

MINIMUM AQUARIUM SIZE: 75 gal. (285 L) or larger.

LIGHTING: Moderate.

WATER: 75-82°F (24-28°C).

FEEDING: *Blastomussa* is photosynthetic but will benefit from regular feedings of meaty foods at night. Offer mysid shrimp, enriched brine shrimp, and other smaller forms of zooplankton.

AQUARIUM COMPATIBILITY: This is a near-perfect community member but vulnerable to attack by other cnidarians. Keep it away from aggressive corals, sea anemones, and mushroom polyps—all potential aggessors.

SPECIAL CARE: Do not locate *Blastomussa* colonies in direct, intense light or strong currents. Cemented to a rocky vertical wall with underwater epoxy, it often does very well. Handle with care as their skeletons are quite fragile.

NOTES: A similar species with smaller corallites, *Blastomussa merletti* (Branched Cup Coral) has smaller polyps. Both are easily propagated by separating the tubular corallite from a robust colony.

PLATE CORAL *Fungia* spp.
(Mushroom Coral, Disc Coral)

OVERVIEW: These are vividly colorful, solitary bottom-dwellers that resemble a mushroom cap or flattened volcano with a central mouth at the peak. They are generally easy to keep, but may roam around a tank.

PHYLUM: Cnidaria (Cnidarians).

NATIVE RANGE: Indo-Pacific.

MAXIMUM SIZE: 12 in. (30 cm).

MINIMUM AQUARIUM SIZE: 75 gal. (285 L).

LIGHTING: Moderate to bright.

WATER: 75–82°F (24–28°C).

FEEDING: *Fungia* spp. are photosynthetic but greedy eaters that need regular feedings of meaty foods such as pieces of marine fish or shrimp placed on the surface of their disk.

AQUARIUM COMPATIBILITY: May kill other sessile invertebrates that it bumps into, exuding a powerfully toxic slime. They may also get the worst end of the deal if they collide with a more aggressive coral. Be sure it has room to wander and that potential victims are elevated or protected by a rocky barrier.

SPECIAL CARE: Each individual *Fungia* is a single polyp and must be handled with great care. If lifting out of the water, gently slide your hand under the skeleton and wait until the coral deflates. If yanked out of the water while still inflated with water, it may tear. Do not place this mobile coral on rockwork.

NOTES: Colors range from tan to pink to green. Small tentacles found over the surface of the animal retract during the day.

PLATE CORAL *Fungia* spp.

Plate corals normally live on sand or rubble and can travel around an aquarium, where they may damage other corals, anemones, and mushroom polyps that are within their reach. To the surprise of many aquarists, *Fungia* spp. may slowly move about the substrate.

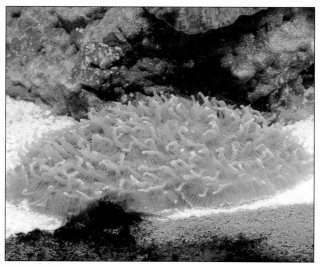

PLATE CORAL *Fungia scutaria*

In the wild, these corals often keep their tentacles retracted during the day. Aquarium specimens may show their tentacles somewhat in daylight, especially if food is available. They will catch and eat meaty foods dropped on their oral disk.

TONGUE CORAL *Herpolitha limax*
(Slipper Coral, Mole Coral)

OVERVIEW: An outstandingly hardy stony coral, this species is an unusual addition to any aquarium, resembling the tongue of a calf or cow in size and shape. (Some colonies fork into Y or X shapes or even bend like a boomerang.) They are much like Plate Corals (*Fungia* spp.), but not nearly as likely to harm tankmates.

PHYLUM: Cnidaria (Cnidarians).

NATIVE RANGE: Indo-Pacific, Red Sea.

MAXIMUM SIZE: 39 in. (1 m).

MINIMUM AQUARIUM SIZE: 100 gal. (380 L).

LIGHTING: Bright.

WATER: 75–82°F (24–28°C).

FEEDING: Tongue and Slipper Corals are photosynthetic but greedy eaters that need regular feedings of meaty foods such as pieces of marine fish or shrimp placed on the animal's surface. It will use its tentacles to move the food morsel to the central groove and into one of its mouths.

AQUARIUM COMPATIBILITY: Needs a sandy or rubble bottom and room to move about. Can be kept in groups and with Plate Corals.

SPECIAL CARE: Handle with care. To lift out of the water, gently slip hand under the animal and wait until it is completely deflated. If raised quickly out of the water while inflated, the polyp may tear.

NOTES: The similar Slipper Coral (*Polyphyllia talpina*) is an equally hardy species with similar habits and requirements. Its central groove is much less pronounced than that of the Tongue Coral (*Herpolitha limax*).

PACIFIC ROSE CORAL *Trachyphyllia radiata*
"Wellsophyllia"

OVERVIEW: Here is very durable open brain coral with a rounded shape, metallic coloration, and close to symmetrical arrangement of its folded mantle. This handsome coral was formerly known as *Wellsophyllia radiata* but is now placed in the same genus as the *Trachyphyllia geoffroyi,* which usually displays an elongated hourglass shape. (Some sources continue to suggest that *T. radiata* is just a variation of *T. geoffroyi*; *Wellsophyllia* fans disagree.)

PHYLUM: Cnidaria (Cnidarians).

NATIVE RANGE: Indo-Pacific.

MAXIMUM SIZE: 12 in. (46 cm).

MINIMUM AQUARIUM SIZE: 30 gal. (114 L).

LIGHTING: Moderate to bright.

WATER: 75–82°F (24–28°C).

FEEDING: *Trachyphyllia* corals are photosynthetic but will benefit from regular feedings of meaty foods at night when the feeding tentacles are extended. Offer minced marine fish, krill, or table shrimp.

AQUARIUM COMPATIBILITY: Keep away from aggressive corals that may attack it with sweeper tentacles. May retract and lose strength if harassed by hermit crabs or fishes that nip at its flesh. Dwarf angelfishes are classic culprits.

SPECIAL CARE: Should be located on a sandy bottom away from strong direct currents that would cover it with substrate.

NOTES: The color of this species is usually a glowing green with white or silvery shading. See the related Open Brain Coral (*Trachyphyllia geoffroyi*), page 92.

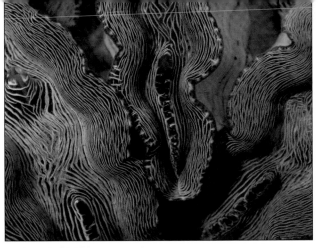

DERASA CLAM *Tridacna derasa*
(Smooth Giant Clam)

OVERVIEW: Once thought of as "the poor man's *Tridacna* Clam," this species makes an excellent choice for beginning invertebrate keepers and is now appearing in much-enhanced color patterns, thanks to captive breeding efforts. This a good clam to start with before investing in more expensive and challenging Maxima and Crocea Clams, which demand very bright metal halide lighting.

PHYLUM: Mollusca (Mollusks).

NATIVE RANGE: Indo-Pacific.

MAXIMUM SIZE: 19 in. (56 cm) long.

MINIMUM AQUARIUM SIZE: 75 gal. (266 L).

LIGHTING: Bright.

WATER: 75–82°F (24–28°C).

FEEDING: The mantle has zooxanthellae that provide the clam with nutrition. Adults will also extract nitrogenous wastes from the water column. Small juveniles under 2 in. (5 cm) need phytoplankton and dissolved nutrients to grow.

AQUARIUM COMPATIBILITY: This is a great reef animal. Some fishes and invertebrates may attack its delicate mantle.

SPECIAL CARE: May be placed on sand or rocky substrate. Avoid buying juveniles with a shell length of less than 4 in. (10 cm), which require special feeding and frequently do not survive in average reef aquarium conditions. Keep calcium levels high for shell growth. Can triple in size in a year's time.

NOTES: Colors vary from tan to green to golden. Always buy aquacultured clams, as these animals are severely overfished in the wild.

GIGAS CLAM *Tridacna gigas*
(Giant Clam)

OVERVIEW: This is the man-killing clam of old thriller movies. In the wild it can live for a century or longer, reaching a shell weight of 500 lbs. (227 kg). Sensationalized stories of giant clams holding the arms or legs of divers until they drowned are discounted by most scientists. For aquarists, this is an interesting, hardy animal that can reach impressive sizes in the aquarium. It requires less-intense lighting than the other species of *Tridacna*.

PHYLUM: Mollusca (Mollusks).

NATIVE RANGE: Indo-Pacific.

MAXIMUM SIZE: Over 4.25 ft. (1.3 m) long.

MINIMUM AQUARIUM SIZE: 180 gal. (684 L).

LIGHTING: Moderate to bright.

WATER: 75–82°F (24–28°C).

FEEDING: The mantle has zooxanthellae that provide the clam with nutrition. Adults will also extract nitrogenous wastes from the water column. Small juveniles under 2 in. (5 cm) need phytoplankton dissolved nutrients to grow.

AQUARIUM COMPATIBILITY: This is a great reef animal. Some fishes and invertebrates may attack its delicate mantle.

SPECIAL CARE: May rest on sand, coral rubble, or hard substrate. Keep calcium levels high for shell growth. Be prepared—in good conditions it can grow very fast.

NOTES: A healthy individual will slap its valves shut when a shadow passes over it. Large clams in shallow aquaria may ejaculate water onto overhanging lights, power cords, and electrical outlets.

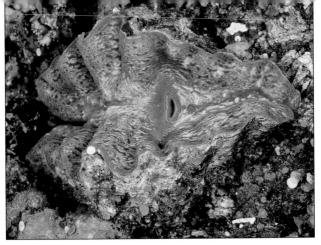

HIPPOPUS CLAM *Hippopus hippopus*
(Horse Hoof Clam, Bear Paw Clam)

OVERVIEW: Once rare in the aquarium trade, this triangular-shelled species of giant clam is becoming more readily available and is extremely hardy. Colors of aquacultured specimens are also becoming more and more attractive, and many sport lime-green striping.

PHYLUM: Mollusca (Mollusks).

NATIVE RANGE: Indo-Pacific.

MAXIMUM SIZE: 16 in. (41 cm) long.

MINIMUM AQUARIUM SIZE: 180 gal. (684 L).

LIGHTING: Bright.

WATER: 75–82°F (24–28°C).

FEEDING: The mantle has zooxanthellae that provide the clam with nutrition. Adults will also extract nitrogenous wastes from the water column. Small juveniles under 2 in. (5 cm) need phytoplankton and dissolved nutrients to grow.

AQUARIUM COMPATIBILITY: Clams are excellent reef community members. Some fishes will attack their soft tissue, but they are less often nipped than the *Tridacna* spp.

SPECIAL CARE: Like *Tridacna* clams, this species needs to be kept out of powerful water currents, which may cause a clam to close and perish. When placing a new clam in the aquarium, be extremely careful not to expose it suddenly to intense light.

NOTES: Place in a bed of sand or coral rubble with room to grow. As with all tridacnids, buy farm-raised specimens rather than wild-caught. When buying a clam, be sure it is responsive: it should close its shell rapidly when your hand creates a shadow over it.

SQUAMOSA CLAM *Tridacna squamosa*
(Fluted Giant Clam, Fluted Clam, Scaly Giant Clam)

OVERVIEW: Often rivaling the beauty of Maxima and Crocea Clams, the Squamosa is easier to keep and can be a long-lived part of a healthy aquarium reefscape. (Maxima and Crocea clams both demand very intense lighting and expert care.)

PHYLUM: Mollusca (Mollusks).

NATIVE RANGE: Indo-Pacific.

MAXIMUM SIZE: About 16 in. (41 cm) long.

MINIMUM AQUARIUM SIZE: 75 gal. (285 L).

LIGHTING: Bright.

WATER: 75–82°F (24–28°C).

FEEDING: The mantle has zooxanthellae that provide the clam with nutrition. Adults will also extract nitrogenous wastes from the water column. Small juveniles under 2 in. (5 cm) need phytoplankton and dissolved nutrients to grow and are more difficult to keep.

AQUARIUM COMPATIBILITY: Clams make great reef community members. Some fishes will attack their soft tissue.

SPECIAL CARE: Clams extract calcium from the aquarium water, and attention must be paid to keeping the calcium level near that of natural seawater: 380 mg/L. Many aquarists aim to keep calcium levels even higher, 400–450 mg/L. Loosely attaches to the rock and may not anchor themselves at all.

NOTES: Place in a bed of sand or among coral rubble with room to grow. Keep away from stinging anemones or aggressive corals that extend sweeper tentacles. As with all tridacnids, buy farm-raised specimens rather than wild-caught.

FIGHTING CONCH *Strombus alatus*
(Florida Fighting Conch)

OVERVIEW: Conchs ("konks") are active herbivores and make interesting additions for many types of marine aquaria. This species is misnamed: it retracts into its shell and sometime gives a startled hop when threatened. Conchs move with a curious lurching motion that is fascinating to watch. They are excellent sand-stirrers.

PHYLUM: Mollusca (Mollusks).

NATIVE RANGE: Caribbean.

MAXIMUM SIZE: 5 in. (13 cm) long.

MINIMUM AQUARIUM SIZE: 50 gal. (190 L).

LIGHTING: Moderate.

WATER: 75–82°F (24–28°C).

FEEDING: Grazes on all sorts of algal growth, diatoms, and detritus. To ensure it is getting enough to eat, offer herbivore pellets.

AQUARIUM COMPATIBILITY: Will ignore fishes and most reef invertebrates to focus on its grazing. May starve in a system with other herbivores competing for food on the substrate. Large hermit crabs will attack and kill juveniles under 1.5 in. (3.8 cm) for their shells.

SPECIAL CARE: Juveniles may climb on rocks and aquarium walls, but adults will mostly graze the open sandy areas. Conchs that climb the walls may be hungry and should be fed. Deep sand bed essential.

NOTES: The shell is brownish to chestnut inside; the outside is drab gray to brown, with small bumps on the rim of each whorl. The body is gray to pale drab green; a pair of large eyes with an evident iris and pupil are visible on tentacles at the front.

QUEEN CONCH *Strombus gigas*
(Pink Conch)

OVERVIEW: Severely overharvested in Florida and much of the Caribbean, this important food animal is making a strong comeback thanks to aquaculture. The captive-bred juveniles make interesting aquarium subjects, with their busy grazing habits and eyestalks constantly surveying the surroundings. However, they get very large and can be like the proverbial "bull in a china shop," toppling unattached corals.

PHYLUM: Mollusca (Mollusks).

NATIVE RANGE: Caribbean.

MAXIMUM SIZE: Up to 16 in. (0.4 m) long.

MINIMUM AQUARIUM SIZE: 180 gal. (684 L).

LIGHTING: Moderate.

WATER: 75–82°F (24–28°C).

FEEDING: Grazes on all sorts of algal growth and diatoms. To ensure it is getting enough to eat, offer herbivore pellets.

AQUARIUM COMPATIBILITY: Good grazer; harmless. Needs a lot of open sand surface area. May starve in a system with other herbivores competing for food on the substrate.

SPECIAL CARE: Juveniles may be kept in small tanks, but they will quickly need more room if properly fed. They must have open sand spaces to graze and will not thrive in a reef aquascape dominated by rock.

NOTES: Oceans Reefs & Aquariums at the Harbor Branch Oceanographic Institution in Ft. Pierce, Florida, pioneered the culturing of both Queen and Fighting Conchs.

RING COWRY *Cypraea annulata*
(Money Cowry)

OVERVIEW: These smaller cowries are excellent, busy grazers and a great addition to the reef aquarium. In the wild they are found in shallow waters and tide pools where water temperatures and salinity levels can shift rapidly and reach extremes that would kill other invertebrates. They are hardy and long-lived if not overstocked and allowed to starve.

PHYLUM: Mollusca (Mollusks).

NATIVE RANGE: Indo-Pacific.

MAXIMUM SIZE: Up to 1 in. (2.5 cm) long.

MINIMUM AQUARIUM SIZE: 10 gal. (38 L) .

LIGHTING: Moderate to bright.

WATER: 75–82°F (24–28°C).

FEEDING: Will graze on all sorts of algal films, filamentous green algae, and diatoms.

AQUARIUM COMPATIBILITY: They are harmless and generally do not bother corals. Hermit crabs in search of new shells may hunt and kill them.

SPECIAL CARE: If these cowries are not getting sufficient food, their diet can be supplemented with herbivore rations, algae flakes, pellets, torn pieces of nori seaweed sheets, and the like.

NOTES: They are considerably smaller than the Tiger Cowry, with shells that range in color from light tan to light green and opalescent white. Golden yellowish brown ring often encircles the shell. A cowry can extend a filmy mantle that may be drab or brightly colored and that bristles with fleshy projections known as papillae.

TIGER COWRY *Cyprea tigris*
(Tiger Shell)

OVERVIEW: Among aquarists, this is the most sought-after of some 200 species of Indo-Pacific cowries. When its mantle is retracted, exposing the lustrous shell, this cowry looks more like creative porcelain art than a snail. It is a hard-working herbivore, easy to keep and long-lived (more than 10 years) in a healthy system where it can find sufficient grazing. This large cowry needs room to roam.

PHYLUM: Mollusca (Mollusks).

NATIVE RANGE: Indo-Pacific.

MAXIMUM SIZE: Up to 6 in. (15 cm).

MINIMUM AQUARIUM SIZE: 75 gal. (285 L).

LIGHTING: Moderate to bright.

WATER: 75–82°F (24–28°C).

FEEDING: It must have algal films, filamentous algae, and/or macroalgae. To ensure that it is being properly nourished, algae flakes, pellets, or pieces of sushi nori (seaweed) can supplement its diet.

AQUARIUM COMPATIBILITY: Will graze on any algae it can find. Do not place in a system already well-stocked with herbivores unless you plan to feed it. Usually benign in reef tank, but an occasional adult will eat large-polyped stony corals, zoanthids, and anemones.

SPECIAL CARE: The aquarium top should be well covered to prevent the cowry from gliding up and out or into the filter system.

NOTES: The Tiger Cowry is one the larger members of its genus. It can prove to be an invertebrate bulldozer, especially in smaller tanks or reefs with loosely arranged rock and corals. The Money or Ring Cowry (opposite page) is a better choice for smaller tanks.

OCTOPUS *Octopus* spp.

(Atlantic Pygmy Octopus, Caribbean Reef Octopus, many others)

OVERVIEW: Some hobbyists consider an octopus as the most interesting and intelligent animal a home aquarist could hope to keep. It requires an aquarium dedicated to its needs and tightly secured to prevent its escape. Be sure to provide plenty of shells, rocky rubble, or even rubber toys; an octopus is curious and playful.

PHYLUM: Mollusca (Mollusks).

NATIVE RANGE: Circumtropical.

MAXIMUM SIZE: 8 in. (20 cm) in diameter.

MINIMUM AQUARIUM SIZE: 30 gal. (114 L).

LIGHTING: Dim to moderate. Octopuses are nocturnal and may be viewed by placing a red light or moon light over the tank. Captive specimens usually become active when the aquarist (and food) are present and will often emerge in dim to moderate light.

WATER: 75–82°F (24–28°C).

FEEDING: A new specimen will require live foods to initiate a feeding response. Offer bait crabs, shrimp, and small marine fishes.

AQUARIUM COMPATIBILITY: Best kept in a species tank. These are highly carnivorous and solitary animals. Keep one per aquarium.

SPECIAL CARE: Requires an aquascape of well-secured rock or PVC pipe and well-oxygenated, clean water. Use a good skimmer and do 25 percent water changes at least every two weeks.

NOTES: The most common species available are *Octopus joubini* (Atlantic Pygmy Octopus); *O. briareus* (Caribbean Reef Octopus); and *O. bimaculatus* (Two-spot Octopus). Natural lifespan of these species is short: no more than two years in the wild.

THORNY OYSTER *Spondylus* spp.
(Atlantic Thorny Oyster, Variable Thorny Oyster, others)

OVERVIEW: A vividly pigmented mantle and numerous small, blue eyes make this an arresting aquarium animal. The Caribbean species is *Spondylus americanus* and has long orange spines covering its shell and a mantle striped in gold, white, and brown. The most common Indo-Pacific species is *Spondylus varians*, shown above, whose mantle may be orange, red, or brown, sometimes mottled.

FAMILY: Mollusca (Mollusks).

NATIVE RANGE: Circumtropical.

MAXIMUM SIZE: 8 in. (20 cm).

MINIMUM AQUARIUM SIZE: 20 gal. (76 L).

LIGHTING: Dim.

WATER: 75–82°F (24–28°C).

FEEDING: Must have daily feedings of phytoplankton and other liquid foods for filter feeders. Turn off filtration and skimming during feeding periods.

AQUARIUM COMPATIBILITY: Not at all aggressive, and rarely pestered by the regular reef-safe fishes (mantle may be nipped by pygmy angles and the odd herbivore that ingests its slime). Other potential predators include large shrimps, lobsters, crabs, and large hermit crabs.

SPECIAL CARE: These oysters typically settle into one spot for life. A new specimen should be placed securely and not moved. Be sure to keep its upper shell oriented toward the surface, as in the wild.

NOTES: These exceptionally beautiful oysters are best kept in a well-established tank. It is imperative that they are fed often.

ABALONE *Haliotis* spp.
(Ear Shells, Sea Ears, Venus Ears, Mutton Shells)

OVERVIEW: Abalones are exotic marine snails, their inner shells coated in nacre or mother-of-pearl and their exterior festooned with sensory tentacles and a row of respiratory ports for expelling water. They are busy aquarium grazers, highly efficient at scouring hard subtrates for algae, diatoms, cyanobacteria, and detritus.

PHYLUM: Mollusca (Mollusks).

NATIVE RANGE: Circumtropical.

MAXIMUM SIZE: 0.8 in. (2.0 cm) to 7.8 in. (20 cm).

MINIMUM AQUARIUM SIZE: 30 gal. (114 L).

LIGHTING: Moderate to bright to foster algae growth.

WATER: 75–82°F (24–28°C).

FEEDING: Abalones are herbivores that require algae-grazing opportunities. They may take herbivore rations—flakes or pellets.

AQUARIUM COMPATIBILITY: Excellent additions to any reef tank. They will not harm corals or other invertebrates.

SPECIAL CARE: Do not attempt to lift or separate an abalone abruptly from the glass or any hard substrate it may be attached to. Its muscular foot adheres tightly to hard surfaces and its shell may tear free of the body. As with many invertebrates, abalones should be carefully acclimated to a new aquarium environment. Avoid abrupt changes in salinity and pH.

NOTES: Captive-bred green abalones are now readily available. Wild-harvested tropical specimens may be red, purple, or other colors. Larger, temperate-water species of abalone are prized for their eating qualities. Be sure to buy only tropical abalone species.

BANDED TROCHUS SNAIL *Trochus* spp.
(Trochus Snail, Top Shell, Turban Snail)

OVERVIEW: With a conical shell rising like a volcano with a distinctively pointed peak, *Trochus* snails are excellent herbivores used for controlling filamentous algae, diatoms, and cyanbacteria films in marine tanks. Many species exist, and distinguishing among them is nearly impossible without expert help. The Banded Trochus is easily recognized by the bands on the shell (they may overgrow with algae in some cases). It is reputed to be one of the best herbivores available today.

PHYLUM: Mollusca (Mollusks).

NATIVE RANGE: Circumtropical.

MAXIMUM SIZE: 1 in. (2.5 cm).

MINIMUM AQUARIUM SIZE: 10 gal. (38 L).

LIGHTING: Moderate to bright—enough to encourage algae growth.

WATER: 75-82°F (24-28°C).

FEEDING: These animals are completely dependent on a diet of grazed algae, diatoms, and cyanobacteria. They can be fed algae flakes and wafers if supplemental feeding is required.

AQUARIUM COMPATIBILITY: Good, peaceful herbivores.

SPECIAL CARE: This snail has no problem uprighting itself if it happens to land on its "back"—*Tectus* spp. (page 112) often do. Do not overstock. The "one snail per gallon" rule is a sure way to end up with starving, dying snails. Add no more than one per 10 gallons and observe how well they are able to keep up with algae growth in your system.

NOTES: *Trochus* species will reproduce successfully if well fed.

CERITH SNAIL *Cerithium litteratum*, others
(Cerith Snails, Ceriths, Stocky Ceriths)

OVERVIEW: Cerith snails have elongate, spire-shaped, attractive shells and they are excellent substrate grazers and scavengers that eat algae, diatoms, cyanobacteria, and uneaten food. In the wild, they are often found in congregations in shallow waters that may number in the hundreds or thousands of snails. These snails are common in the Caribbean and South Florida.

PHYLUM: Mollusca (Mollusks).

NATIVE RANGE: Caribbean. (Genus is circumtropical.)

MAXIMUM SIZE: 1.25 in. (3 cm).

MINIMUM AQUARIUM SIZE: 10 gal. (38 L).

LIGHTING: Moderate to bright—enough to encourage algae growth.

WATER: 75–82°F (24–28°C).

FEEDING: Ceriths are scavengers that work the substrate for all forms of algae and detritus—anything edible. If grazing is scant, they can be fed algae flakes or herbivore rations.

AQUARIUM COMPATIBILITY: Harmless with corals and good reef aquarium animals.

SPECIAL CARE: Acclimate slowly. Do not overstock these, or any other herbivorous snails or hermit crabs. If introduced in large numbers (one snail per gallon is sometimes recklessly recommended), many will starve once the algae problem is under control. One per 10 gal. (38 L) is a more reasonable stocking rule.

NOTES: These, and most other algae-grazing snails, may be killed by hermit crabs. The aquarist may want to choose between stocking hermits or snails for algae control.

NERITE *Nerita* spp.
(Zebra Nerite, Checker Nerite, Bleeding Tooth, others)

OVERVIEW: Nerites are active algae grazers and can make good herbivores for the reef or "mostly fish" aquarium. The best species stay underwater, while those collected in tide pools and mangrove swamps may live near the high-water line and emerge to breathe.

PHYLUM: Mollusca (Mollusks).

NATIVE RANGE: Circumtropical.

MAXIMUM SIZE: Up to 1.5 in. (3.8 cm) long.

MINIMUM AQUARIUM SIZE: Nano tanks, 2 gal. (8 L) or larger.

LIGHTING: Moderate to bright—enough to encourage algae growth.

WATER: 75–82°F (24–28°C).

FEEDING: Will graze on filamentous green algae, diatoms, and cyanobacterial films in nocturnal feeding sessions.

AQUARIUM COMPATIBILITY: Good aquarium animals. Hermit crabs may kill them for their shells.

SPECIAL CARE: Do not overstock. One snail per 10 gallons is a safe rule of thumb. Snails will starve if too many are introduced at the first sign of an algae problem. Most are long-lived animals and should not be misused. If you suspect your snails are starving, return some to the aquarium shop or give them away. Nerites will often glide up and out of the tank. Avoid buying nerites that are clustered above the water's surface; those species spend most of their lives out of the water.

NOTES: There are numerous species of nerites in tropical seas. Many have dull, muted colors, but a few, such as the Zebra Nerite from the Caribbean, are white with striking black patterns.

PYRAMID TOP SHELL *Tectus* spp.
(Tectus Snails)

OVERVIEW: With a conical shell rising into a distinctively pointed peak, the top shells are excellent herbivores used for controlling filamentous algae, diatoms, and cyanobacterial films in marine tanks. Distinguishing among the many species is nearly impossible without expert help. *Tectus fenestratus* is an attractive Indo-Pacific species being aquacultured for the aquarium trade and sold as a Turban Snail. Some species grow too large for smaller aquariums.

PHYLUM: Mollusca (Mollusks).

NATIVE RANGE: Circumtropical.

MAXIMUM SIZE: 3 in. (7.6 cm).

MINIMUM AQUARIUM SIZE: 10 gal. (38 L).

LIGHTING: Moderate to bright—enough to encourage algae growth.

WATER: 75–82°F (24–28°C).

FEEDING: These animals are completely dependent on a diet of grazed algae, diatoms, and cyanobacteria. They can be fed algae flakes and wafers if supplemental feeding is required.

AQUARIUM COMPATIBILITY: Good, peaceful herbivores.

SPECIAL CARE: These snails are sensitive to sudden changes in salinity. May have difficulty uprighting if they land upside down in the sand. Do not overstock. The "one snail per gallon" rule is a sure way to end up with starving, dying snails.

NOTES: *Tectus* species are easily confused with *Trochus* snails that have more distinct spiral ridges, like a shell made of coiled string. *Tectus* species will reproduce successfully in the aquarium if kept well fed.

SAND SNAIL *Nassarius* spp.
(Nassa Snails)

OVERVIEW: They aren't necessarily the prettiest of snails (they have been likened to olive pits), but these small whelks can live for decades if properly maintained. They are especially good at scavenging uneaten food before it decays and will burrow into the substrate, keeping it well groomed and free of anaerobic zones.

PHYLUM: Mollusca (Mollusks).

NATIVE RANGE: Circumtropical.

MAXIMUM SIZE: 1 in. (2.5 cm).

MINIMUM AQUARIUM SIZE: 10 gal. (38 L).

LIGHTING: Moderate to bright—enough to encourage algae growth.

WATER: 75–82°F (24–28°C).

FEEDING: They will find and consume leftover meaty fish foods. To feed them intentionally, offer adult brine shrimp, mysid shrimp, shredded marine fish, or shrimp flesh.

AQUARIUM COMPATIBILITY: They are harmless scavengers and fit into most marine aquariums without problem. Hermit crabs may hunt and kill them for their shells.

SPECIAL CARE: Do not overstock. They will starve if too many are placed in a system. Ignore the all-too-common "rule" of one snail per gallon; start with one per 10 gallons. Think twice about buying a "cleanup crew" that mixes snails and hermit crabs, as the crabs may eventually prey on the snails.

NOTES: In good conditions with ample feeding opportunities, they will lay spiraling clusters of eggs on the aquarium walls. These will hatch and release planktonic larvae, which usually do not survive.

STAR SHELL *Astraea* spp.
(Astrea Snail, West Indian Star Shell)

OVERVIEW: These are among the best grazing snails for marine aquariums. The species collected for aquarium use are a good size, not too large, and they can be long-lived if not allowed to starve. Their shells often become encrusted with pink, red, and purple coralline algae, making them especially attractive in a reef aquarium.

PHYLUM: Mollusca (Mollusks).

NATIVE RANGE: Circumtropical.

MAXIMUM SIZE: 1.5 in. (3.8 cm).

MINIMUM AQUARIUM SIZE: Nano tanks, 2 gal. (8L).

LIGHTING: Moderate to bright—enough to encourage algae growth.

WATER: 75–82°F (24–28°C).

FEEDING: These animals are completely dependent on a diet of grazed algae, diatoms, and cyanobacteria. They can be fed algae flakes and wafers if supplemental feeding is required.

AQUARIUM COMPATIBILITY: These are peaceful community members with no interest in corals or other sessile invertebrates. They may be killed by hermit crabs looking for a meal and a new shell.

SPECIAL CARE: Acclimate slowly. Do not overstock these or any other herbivorous snails or hermit crabs. One per 10 gal. (38 L) is a reasonable stocking rule. May have difficulty uprighting themselves if they are upended and will need to be turned over.

NOTES: Shell shape is less pointed than *Tectus* and *Trochus* species. When viewed from above or below, there may be projecting spines around the base of the shell, giving the suggestion of a starburst.

TURBO GRAZER *Turbo* spp.
(Turbo Snail)

OVERVIEW: Turbo Grazers are mainstays in the arsenal of biocontrols aquarium keepers can use to cope with algae growth. If collected from tropical waters, they are generally long-lived and good at grazing filamentous green algae, diatoms, and cyanobacteria. Always buy from a reputable source. Some Turbo Grazers collected on the shores of Baja California come from subtropical conditions and never prove to be hardy in warm-water aquariums.

PHYLUM: Mollusca (Mollusks).

NATIVE RANGE: Circumtropical.

MAXIMUM SIZE: 6 in. (15 cm).

MINIMUM AQUARIUM SIZE: 10 gal. (38 L).

LIGHTING: Moderate to bright—enough to encourage algae growth.

WATER: 75–82°F (24–28°C).

FEEDING: These animals are completely dependent on a diet of grazed algae, diatoms, and cyanobacteria. They can be fed algae flakes and wafers if supplemental feeding is required.

AQUARIUM COMPATIBILITY: They are dedicated herbivores. Some do get too large for smaller aquariums and can bulldoze a nano-scale aquascape. They may have difficulty uprighting themselves.

SPECIAL CARE: Do not overstock.

NOTES: The so-called Mini-Turbos or "Baby Grazing Snails" (*Collonista* spp.) are a different genus entirely, but they do make excellent herbivores in all size reef aquariums. Their small size (1/4 in. or 6 mm) allows them to work in and out of tight spaces. They have light-colored shells and will reproduce in most aquariums.

COCO WORM *Protula magnifica*
(Magnificent Feather Duster, Hard-tube Feather Duster)

OVERVIEW: This species needs an aquarium that has high levels of calcium and regular infusions of small phytoplankton. Given these conditions, it is capable of a long life.

CLASS: Polychaeta (Polychaete Worms).

NATIVE RANGE: Tropical seas.

MAXIMUM SIZE: Tentacle crown to 3 in. (7.6 cm) in diameter; large tube to almost 1 in. (2.5 cm) in diameter in a large adult; may be more than 24 in. (61 cm) long.

MINIMUM AQUARIUM SIZE: Small tanks, 10 gal. (38 L) or larger.

LIGHTING: Moderate.

WATER: 75–82°F (24–28°C).

FEEDING: Requires daily offerings of very fine particulate foods, phytoplankton, and high-quality filter-feeder rations. Feeds on particulate organic material and phytoplankton in the wild. Be prepared to provide ready supply of phytoplankton.

AQUARIUM COMPATIBILITY: Best kept only by aquarists willing to invest the money and time to meet its nutritional needs. Captive specimens generally will starve to death over a period of about six months to a year with improper diet.

SPECIAL CARE: Strong to moderate currents are necessary.

NOTES: The tentacle crown is comprised of two helices of three or four whorls. The tentacle stalks and the shafts of each "feather" tend to be red, hot pink, or rose-peach. The feather filaments are usually white or occasionally pink. The Coco Worm lacks the plug, or operculum, common to many serpulids.

GIANT FEATHER DUSTER WORM *Sabellastarte* **spp.**
(Soft-tube Feather Duster)

OVERVIEW: When it comes to long-term husbandry, this polycheate has a dubious reputation. With the ready supply of phytoplankton available to hobbyists now, its care requirements can be met by the determined hobbyist.

CLASS: Polychaeta (Polychaete Worms).

NATIVE RANGE: Indo-Pacific.

MAXIMUM SIZE: 4 in. (10 cm).

MINIMUM AQUARIUM SIZE: 10 gal. (38 L).

LIGHTING: Moderate.

WATER: 75–82°F (24–28°C).

FEEDING: Feeds on particulate organic material and phytoplankton. Requires regular daily target feeding under the feeding crown, not in the middle of the structure.

AQUARIUM COMPATIBILITY: Sometimes eaten by crustaceans and sea urchins (the latter have been known to chew through the sedimentary tubes of sabellids).

SPECIAL CARE: Drill hole in live rock or find appropriate interstice to place the worm tube. Never purchase an individual that has crawled completely or even partially out of its tube. The Giant Feather Duster Worm may do better in tanks with greater organic loads to help supplement its diet.

NOTES: The body tube, which is created by the worm, is comprised of sand grains and mucous in many sabellids. They are found buried under the substrate, with only the top of the tube projecting, or projecting from holes in hard surfaces.

EMERALD CRAB *Mithraculus sculptus*
(Green Clinging Crab, Spider Crab, Hard-back Crab)

OVERVIEW: These interesting little Caribbean crabs are often found hugging the substrate where they greedily forage all sorts of algae and plants. The Emerald Crab is prized as one of the few biocontrols for *Valonia* and *Ventricaria* bubble algae, dreaded nuisances that can overrun an aquarium, choking out corals and other sessile invertebrates on the rocky substrate. Unlike most of its kin, the Emerald Crab neither decorates itself nor preys very often on living animals.

PHYLUM: Arthropoda (Arthropods).

NATIVE RANGE: Caribbean.

MAXIMUM SIZE: 2 in. (5 cm) wide.

MINIMUM AQUARIUM SIZE: 10 gal. (38 L).

LIGHTING: Dim to bright.

WATER: 75–82°F (24–28°C).

FEEDING: Omnivorous, but primarily an herbivore. It will scavenge uneaten fish food. Unlike most other crabs, it will rarely hunt and kill fishes or other invertebrates.

AQUARIUM COMPATIBILITY: Generally considered reef safe, but it has been reported to snatch and eat unwary or resting small fishes. May eat some types of branching coralline algae.

SPECIAL CARE: Should not be overstocked, even when a plague of algae needs to be controlled. Let one or two crabs do the work, and add more only if the grazing will support them.

NOTES: *Mithraculus sculptus* requires normal reef aquarium conditions, plenty of algae, and some rockwork, but is otherwise undemanding. Formerly known as *Mithrax sculptus*.

POM POM CRAB *Lybia* spp.
(Boxer Crab)

OVERVIEW: Another fascinating case of symbiosis, this crab holds small sea anemones in its pinchers and waves them at a potential threat as if it is boxing. It may also use its "pom poms" to collect detritus, which it then feeds on. It is attractively marked, with striped legs and bold markings on its carapace. The anemones are dropped during molting but are retrieved once this process is complete.

PHYLUM: Arthropoda (Arthropods).

NATIVE RANGE: Indo-Pacific.

MAXIMUM SIZE: 0.6 in. (1.5 cm).

MINIMUM AQUARIUM SIZE: 2 gal. (8 L).

LIGHTING: Dim.

WATER: 75–82°F (24–28°C).

FEEDING: Omnivore. Will feed on detritus and small food particles that it picks off the substrate or that adhere to its anemone partner. Should attempt to target feed with finely chopped, meaty foods.

AQUARIUM COMPATIBILITY: Reef safe, but in a larger aquarium it is likely to disappear. Prone to being eaten by a number of carnivorous fish species, but some may be deterred by its stinging anemones. Large dottybacks, hawkfishes, wrasses, sand perches, and puffers may attack them. It will not harm any of its tankmates.

SPECIAL CARE: A cryptic species that must be provided with rubble, rocks, and crevices to hide under or in. If well cared for, it will live for several years in captivity.

NOTES: There are at least two species that enter the trade: *Lybia tesselata* (Indo-Pacific) and *L. edmondsoni* (Hawaiian Islands).

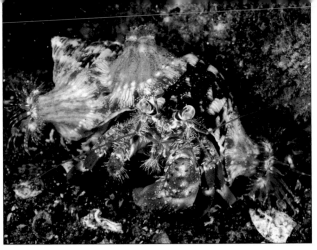

ANEMONE HERMIT CRAB *Dardanus pedunculatus*

OVERVIEW: This genus of large hermits is not suitable for the reef aquarium. Nonetheless, they are fascinating pets and great scavengers that will do well in a species tank or if housed with larger fishes. This particular species is unique in that it sticks small sea anemones to its shell to provide further protection from predators. (See also page 159 in Invertebrates to Avoid.)

PHYLUM: Arthropoda (Arthropods).

NATIVE RANGE: Indo-Pacific.

MAXIMUM SIZE: 4 in. (10 cm).

MINIMUM AQUARIUM SIZE: 15 gal. (38 L).

LIGHTING: Dim to moderate (higher light levels may ensure anemone survival).

WATER: 75–82°F (24–28°C).

FEEDING: Omnivore. Will graze on filamentous algae, cyanobacteria, leftover food, defenseless invertebrates, and small fishes. In order to insure survival of anemone associates, target-feed them finely chopped seafood (e.g., shrimp).

AQUARIUM COMPATIBILITY: This species may harass coral polyps, clams, zoanthids, and other vulnerable invertebrates and kill snails. Can be kept with heavily armored crustaceans and larger fishes.

SPECIAL CARE: Keep singly or in pairs if you have a larger tank (100 gallons or larger) as individuals may battle for shell rights.

NOTES: Once acclimated, these hermit crabs can be long-lived in the aquarium. Larger specimens will require fairly sizable shells. When it changes shells, it relocates the anemones on its new home!

BLUE-EYE HERMIT CRAB *Paguristes sericeus*

OVERVIEW: Although not at all reef safe, this and other large members of its genus make colorful, fascinating pets and great scavengers in tanks with larger fishes and invertebrates that can fend for themselves. Bigger hermit crabs can also be kept in a species tank devoted to them alone, or perhaps with a large damsel or a big, aggressive dottyback. These crabs have prominent eyes that are a brilliant blue, orange in overall color, hairy legs and a pair of large claws. (See also page 159 in Invertebrates to Avoid.)

PHYLUM: Arthropoda (Arthropods).

NATIVE RANGE: South Florida, Bahamas, Caribbean.

MAXIMUM SIZE: 2.5 in. (6 cm).

MINIMUM AQUARIUM SIZE: 10 gal. (38 L).

LIGHTING: Dim.

WATER: 75–82°F (24–28°C).

FEEDING: Omnivore. Will graze on filamentous algae, cyanobacteria, leftover food, defenseless invertebrates, and small fishes. If kept in a tank without fishes, offer it meaty foods several times per week.

AQUARIUM COMPATIBILITY: Never add a larger hermit to a reef aquarium. It will attack coral polyps, clams, and any other vulnerable invertebrate. Can be kept with other robust crustaceans and larger fishes. May fight with other large hermits for shells.

SPECIAL CARE: They are amazing scavengers—make sure some food gets to them.

NOTES: Once acclimated, these hermit crabs can be long-lived in the aquarium. Larger specimens will require fairly sizable shells.

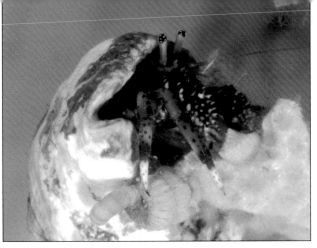

BLUE-LEG HERMIT CRAB *Clibanarius tricolor*
(Tricolor Hermit Crab, Red-White-and-Blue Hermit Crab)

OVERVIEW: This is an attractive hermit crab, constantly scuttling around the aquarium in search of food. It is primarily bought for its ability to graze filamentous algae and cyanobacteria, but it is an omnivore that will help in cleaning up uneaten food and other detritus. To the dismay of some, it may attack and consume small snails and then take over their shells.

PHYLUM: Arthropoda (Arthropods).

NATIVE RANGE: Caribbean.

MAXIMUM SIZE: About 1.0 in. (2.5 cm).

MINIMUM AQUARIUM SIZE: 2 gal. (8 L).

LIGHTING: Dim.

WATER: 75–82°F (24–28°C).

FEEDING: Omnivore. In tanks without sufficient algal growth, offer seaweed flakes, pellets, or nori several times weekly.

AQUARIUM COMPATIBILITY: Likely to kill algae-grazing snails (e.g., *Astraea*). May pick at various polyps, but is generally regarded as reef safe unless food is scarce.

SPECIAL CARE: Do not overstock hermit crabs. After cleaning up an algae problem, the population often loses members (or starts to attack other invertebrates) unless they are intentionally fed. Add one per 10 gallons.

NOTES: When keeping hermit crabs, be sure to have a selection of empty shells in the tank so they can "trade up" as they grow. Most good aquarium shops can supply reef rubble with shells of various sizes.

CONE SHELL HERMIT CRAB *Ciliopagurus strigatus*
(Halloween Hermit Crab, Striped Hermit Crab)

OVERVIEW: Here is a glorious and distinctive hermit crab that is typically found in the shell of a *Conus* sp. snail, a huge genus that includes some of the deadliest invertebrates known (see page 167). In a reef aquarium, it may eat small clams, shrimp, feather duster worms, and soft-bodied corals. Placed in a community of fishes, it would add interest and act as a valuable scavenger.

PHYLUM: Arthropoda (Arthropods).

NATIVE RANGE: Indo-Pacific, most imported from Hawaii.

MAXIMUM SIZE: 2 in. (5 cm).

MINIMUM AQUARIUM SIZE: 4 gal. (16 L).

LIGHTING: Dim.

WATER: 75–82°F (24–28°C).

FEEDING: Omnivore. If scavenging opportunities are limited, offer dried seaweed and meaty foods such as chopped shrimp or pieces of marine fish such as silversides.

AQUARIUM COMPATIBILITY: Dubious reef-tank selection—some report no problems keeping with corals. Best kept with fishes and rugged invertebrates that can fend for themselves. May kill snails for their shells, but most often utilize cone snail shells.

SPECIAL CARE: Avoid keeping it with triggerfish, puffers, and very large wrasses that will target and may eventually eat it.

NOTES: This species has an extremely flat body that seems perfectly adapted to the tight aperture of an empty cone shell. Cone shells are highly collectible, and empty shells can be found at shell shops and from Internet sellers.

DWARF ZEBRA HERMIT CRAB *Calcinus seurati*
(Dwarf Zebra Reef Hermit, White-banded Hermit Crab)

OVERVIEW: This is one of the best hermit crab grazers, staying relatively small and eating filamentous algae, red slime algae, and usually ignoring reef invertebrates. Its left claw is enlarged and it has bright blue eyes on blue and orange eyestalks with orange antennae. Its claws are white or light colored.

PHYLUM: Arthropoda (Arthropods).

NATIVE RANGE: Indo-West Pacific, Hawaii.

MAXIMUM SIZE: 1 in. (2.5 cm).

MINIMUM AQUARIUM SIZE: Nano tanks, 2 gal. (8 L).

LIGHTING: Dim.

WATER: 75–82°F (24–28°C).

FEEDING: Omnivore. Will usually confine itself to grazing and scavenging uneaten food. If algae becomes scarce, it may need to be fed dried seaweed flakes or reef rations for fishes.

AQUARIUM COMPATIBILITY: This is a good reef animal. When it needs larger space, like all hermit crabs, it may kill and eat a snail and then move into its new shell. Provide a variety of sizes of empty snail shells in the tank for best husbandry.

SPECIAL CARE: Do not stock more than one hermit crab per 10 gallons. Hermit crabs often starve once a plague of algae is brought under control.

NOTES: This species is often sold as and confused with *Calcinus levimanus*, which does not have the distinctive black-and-white banded legs. This is the more attractive of the two species. Both are sometimes sold as the Hawaiian Zebra Hermit Crab.

ELECTRIC BLUE HERMIT CRAB *Calcinus elegans*
(Blue-knuckle Hermit Crab)

OVERVIEW: Here is one of the most colorful of the common aquarium hermit crabs, with jet black legs banded in bright blue to match its eyestalks. It is primarily bought for its ability to graze filamentous algae and cyanobacteria, but it is an omnivore that will help in cleaning up uneaten food and other detritus. While it does not cause excessive problems in the reef tank, it is not as benign as *Paguristes cadenati* (see page 128).

PHYLUM: Arthropoda (Arthropods).

NATIVE RANGE: Indo-Pacific.

MAXIMUM SIZE: 2 in. (5 cm).

MINIMUM AQUARIUM SIZE: 4 gal. (16 L).

LIGHTING: Dim.

WATER: 75–82°F (24–28°C).

FEEDING: Omnivore. In tanks without sufficient algal growth, offer seaweed flakes, pellets, or nori several times weekly.

AQUARIUM COMPATIBILITY: Likely to kill algae-grazing snails and may damage tube worms. Generally regarded as one of the reef-safe hermit crab grazers.

SPECIAL CARE: Do not overstock hermit crabs (add one per 10 gallons of aquarium volume). After cleaning up an algae problem, the population often dwindles unless they are intentionally fed.

NOTES: When keeping hermit crabs, be sure to have a selection of empty shells in the tank so that they can "trade up" as they grow. Most good aquarium shops can supply reef rubble with shells of various sizes.

POLKA-DOT HERMIT CRAB *Phimochirus opercularus*
(Caribbean Hermit Crab)

OVERVIEW: This is an energetic algae-grazing crab, always seemingly busy, and attractively pigmented with orange legs, blue eyes, and a red body with white splotches. It uses its large claw as a substitute operculum to cover the opening of its snail shell when it is withdrawn. (Operculum means "little lid" and is used by live snails to seal their shells shut to exclude predators.) Will help control filamentous algae and cyanobacteria in the aquarium.

PHYLUM: Arthropoda (Arthropods).

NATIVE RANGE: Caribbean, tropical Western Atlantic.

MAXIMUM SIZE: 2 in. (5 cm).

MINIMUM AQUARIUM SIZE: 4 gal. (16 L).

LIGHTING: Moderate to bright.

WATER: 75–82°F (24–28°C).

FEEDING: Omnivore. In tanks without sufficient algal growth, offer seaweed flakes, pellets, or nori several times weekly.

AQUARIUM COMPATIBILITY: Will kill algae-grazing snails to take their shells. Territorial and aggressive toward its own species. Keep singly in small tanks.

SPECIAL CARE: Do not overstock hermit crabs. After cleaning up an algae problem, the population often dwindles unless they are intentionally fed. They are long-lived if not starved.

NOTES: When keeping hermit crabs, be sure to have a selection of empty shells in the tank so that they can "trade up" as they grow. Most good aquarium shops can supply reef rubble with shells of various sizes.

ELECTRIC ORANGE HERMIT CRAB *Calcinus* sp.

OVERVIEW: This attractive hermit has bright orange-banded legs and blue eyes on blue stalks, and not only is it eye-catching, but it earns its keep by scavenging and feeding on pest algae and cyanobacteria. It is larger than some of the other algae-eating hermits and is more of a threat to small fishes and snails. If underfed, it may even eat the occasional cnidarian polyp.

PHYLUM: Arthropoda (Arthropods).

NATIVE RANGE: Indo-Pacific.

MAXIMUM SIZE: .8 in. (2 cm).

MINIMUM AQUARIUM SIZE: Nano tanks, 2 gal. (8 L).

LIGHTING: Dim.

WATER: 75–82°F (24–28°C).

FEEDING: Omnivore. If algae becomes scarce, it may need to be fed dried seaweed flakes or reef rations for fishes.

AQUARIUM COMPATIBILITY: A relatively passive species, but may cause problems if not well fed. Do not keep it with hawkfishes, large wrasses, triggers, puffers, or porcupinefishes. More than one can be kept in the same tank, but do not overstock, as they will fight for shells and food. The Electric Orange Hermit will pull snails from their shells and commandeer their armored homes.

SPECIAL CARE: Like other hermits, this crab is good at keeping the upper layer of the sand bed stirred and "processing" food and organic wastes that end up behind the reef decor.

NOTES: Provide a collection of shells as numerous choices of housing as it grows. It has two equal-sized white-tipped claws.

SCARLET HERMIT CRAB *Paguristes cadenati*
(Red-Leg Hermit Crab)

OVERVIEW: With bright red or scarlet legs and beady eyes on yellow stalks, this is an interesting animal and an excellent forager on filamentous nuisance algae. It will pluck algae from hard-to-reach places, including among the branches of stony corals. It will feed on cyanobacteria and will scavenge fish foods.

PHYLUM: Arthropoda (Arthropods).

NATIVE RANGE: Caribbean, Tropical Western Atlantic.

MAXIMUM SIZE: 1.5 in. (3.75 cm).

MINIMUM AQUARIUM SIZE: Nano tanks, 2 gal. (8 L).

LIGHTING: Dim.

WATER: 75–82°F (24–28°C).

FEEDING: Omnivore. If algae becomes scarce, it may need to be fed dried seaweed flakes or reef rations for fishes.

AQUARIUM COMPATIBILITY: If overstocked and hungry, these (and most hermit crabs) may attack snails, coral polyps, and any vulnerable invertebrate. When it needs larger home, it may kill and eat a snail and then move into its new shell. That said, it is one of the best reef-tank hermits.

SPECIAL CARE: Do not stock more than one hermit crab per 10 gallons. They will compete for food with serpent stars and scavenging snails.

NOTES: This species is primarily nocturnal. To help avoid predation on your snail population, provide a collection of shells or shell rubble so that it has numerous choices of housing as it grows. Empty snail shell assortments are available from aquarium suppliers.

YELLOW HAIRY HERMIT CRAB *Aniculus maximus*
(Hawaiian Yellow Hairy Hermit Crab)

OVERVIEW: This an animal that could decimate a reef aquarium, but it is so attractive and interesting to watch that it deserves a tank of its own. It may also be kept in a mostly fish-only aquarium with large, active species that aren't in danger of being caught. However, this crustacean has been known to capture torpid fish at night. It is the hairiest hermit crab known, with richly pigmented yellow or golden legs tinged with red. (See also page 159 in Invertebrates to Avoid.)

PHYLUM: Arthropoda (Arthropods).

NATIVE RANGE: Indo-Pacific.

MAXIMUM SIZE: 6 in. (15 cm).

MINIMUM AQUARIUM SIZE: 30 gal. (114 L).

LIGHTING: Dim.

WATER: 75–82°F (24–28°C).

FEEDING: Omnivore. Will graze on filamentous algae, leftover food, defenseless invertebrates, and small fishes.

AQUARIUM COMPATIBILITY: A threat to most invertebrates and smaller fishes. It eat coral polyps, clams, anemones, and even echinoderms. Must be housed with larger fishes that can fend for themselves.

SPECIAL CARE: Stock singly. In the wild, it often lives in caves or under ledges in spaces large enough to accommodate its shell. Needs clean, well-filtered water kept in constant circulation.

NOTES: Larger specimens are sometimes found in Triton's Trumpet Shells, as well as *Turbo* snail shells. Bigger shells may be required as the crab grows. These animals can live for years in the aquarium.

BLUE SPINY LOBSTER *Panulirus versicolor*
(Pacific Spiny Lobster, Painted Lobster)

OVERVIEW: Gourmets love them with drawn butter, but juveniles of this and other lobster species make interesting, easy-to-keep aquarium subjects. They are not reef safe, but will do well in a community of fishes that does not include small bottom dwellers. This is among the most beautiful of all lobsters, with vibrant shades of blue in its tail and contrasting black and white striping, a green body, and elegant white antennae.

PHYLUM: Arthropoda (Arthropods).

NATIVE RANGE: Indo-Pacific.

MAXIMUM SIZE: 14 in. (36 cm) body length.

MINIMUM AQUARIUM SIZE: 100 gal. (380 L).

LIGHTING: Dim.

WATER: 75–82°F (24–28°C).

FEEDING: Omnivore. Offer a variety of meaty foods such as pieces of marine fish, shrimp, and squid.

AQUARIUM COMPATIBILITY: Lobsters are lethal predators. They are likely to ignore most corals but will eat clams, ornamental shrimps, snails, hermit crabs, urchins, and fishes they can catch. Smaller lobsters may grab fishes that "sleep" in caves, while full-grown lobsters are a threat to most fishes, although less so in very large systems.

SPECIAL CARE: Must have one or more caves or ledges that provide shelter where it can hide. Keep singly; they sometimes eat each other.

NOTES: The Caribbean Spiny Lobster (*Panulirus argus*) is less brightly colored but equally delicious.

REEF LOBSTER *Enoplometopus* spp.
(Flame Lobster)

OVERVIEW: Gloriously pigmented, these are the marine equivalent of freshwater crayfish, and they make very hardy aquarium animals. Colors range from orange to deep red, lavender, or deep purple with orange legs. These modestly sized lobsters are generally reef safe, with their claws used mostly for defense. They mostly feed at night in the wild and may tend to stay hiding in the shadows when the lights are on.

PHYLUM: Arthropoda (Arthropods).

NATIVE RANGE: Circumtropical.

MAXIMUM SIZE: 6 in. (15 cm) long; most smaller.

MINIMUM AQUARIUM SIZE: 20 gal. (114 L).

LIGHTING: Dim.

WATER: 75–82°F (24–28°C).

FEEDING: Omnivore. Will scavenge all manner of foods and wastes. Offer a variety of meaty items such as pieces of marine fish, shrimp, and squid.

AQUARIUM COMPATIBILITY: If kept well fed, will ignore most reef invertebrates and fishes. However, when placed in a nano tank crowded with reef invertebrates, they may prove destructive.

SPECIAL CARE: They need a sand bed for burrowing and good water conditions: clean, well-filtered, and with vigorous circulation.

NOTES: Debelius' Reef Lobster (*Enoplometopus debelius*) is an outstanding choice for a species tank with a cave or two and perhaps a fish or two that hover in the water column, such as larger cardinal-fishes. (See photo, page 180.)

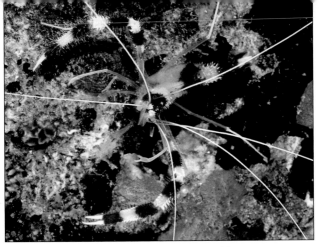

BANDED CORAL SHRIMP *Stenopus hispidus*
(Boxer Shrimp, Coral Banded Shrimp, Barber Pole Shrimp)

OVERVIEW: With two pairs of long, graceful antennae and a set of claws that it raises in what appears to be a pugilistic stance, this is a fascinating animal and great beginner's invertebrate. It will clean parasites and detritus from the skin and mouth of larger fish species. In the aquarium, it is a good scavenger but can be aggressive toward other crustaceans.

PHYLUM: Arthropoda (Arthropods).

NATIVE RANGE: Circumtropical.

MAXIMUM SIZE: 2.4 in. (6 cm).

MINIMUM AQUARIUM SIZE: 20 gal. (76 L).

LIGHTING: Dim.

WATER: 75–82°F (24–28°C).

FEEDING: Scavenger. Will hunt and eat bristleworms, and catches meaty fish foods that drift by in the water column.

AQUARIUM COMPATIBILITY: Always buy one *Stenopus* shrimp or a mated pair that you have witnessed living together. Unpaired shrimp will fight to the death. In tight quarters, they may attack other shrimps and crabs. While rare, adults may eat small fishes.

SPECIAL CARE: A pair will regularly produce eggs, seen as a green mass under the female's belly. Larvae will be eaten by other inhabitants of the system and will survive only with special feeding.

NOTES: This species of cleaner shrimp molts and sheds its exoskeletons periodically and easily loses and regrows claws. Vulnerable to some fish just after molting, including dottybacks, hawkfishes, and wrasses. Will eat their own chiton-rich molt.

GOLDEN CORAL SHRIMP *Stenopus scutellatus*
This is a small, attractive Caribbean boxer shrimp, with behaviors and care identical to the Banded Coral Shrimp. Reef fishes recognize the long antennae of cleaner shrimps as an invitation to approach and be groomed.

YELLOW BANDED CORAL SHRIMP *Stenopus zanzibaricus*
This is one of several related Indo-Pacific species, including the beautiful blue and purple *Stenopus tenuirostris*. Note "dukes up" white claws, likely regenerating after the previous pair were lost in a fight or in an attack by a predator.

CAMELBACK SHRIMP *Rhynchocinetes* spp.
(Hingebeak Prawn, Dancing Shrimp, Candy Shrimp, Camel Shrimp)

OVERVIEW: There are numerous species of these humpbacked shrimps, many with bright red-and-white colors and large eyes. Kept in groups, they make an interesting sight, and they provide good scavenging services, searching out and eating all manner of uneaten food and detritus. The Camelback is also known to eat certain soft coral polyps and zoanthids—reef aquarists beware. A safer prospect is the Peppermint Shrimp, page 140.

PHYLUM: Arthropoda (Arthropods).

NATIVE RANGE: Circumtropical.

MAXIMUM SIZE: 1 to 2.5 in. (2.5 to 6.5 cm).

MINIMUM AQUARIUM SIZE: Nano tanks, 2 gal. (8 L).

LIGHTING: Dim.

WATER: 75-82°F (24-28°C).

FEEDING: Scavengers and carnivores. Will take mysid shrimp, adult brine shrimp, minced fish, and shrimp flesh.

AQUARIUM COMPATIBILITY: Will ignore fishes and other crustaceans. It may attack mushroom corals, zoanthids, star polyps, and leather corals.

SPECIAL CARE: These shrimp form large aggregations in the wild and are best kept in groups of at least three to five individuals. Males will sometimes fight; it's best to keep one male and several females. (Males have larger pinchers; female pictured above.) They are naturally nocturnal and need a cave or overhanging ledge to hide.

NOTES: Their bulbous compound eyes appear blue, green, or black in the daylight, but reflect as glowing red or copper.

CLOWN ANEMONE SHRIMP *Periclimenes brevicarpalis*
(Pizza Anemone Shrimp)

OVERVIEW: This is one of a number of shrimps that associate with sea anemones, especially the so-called Pizza Anemone (*Cryptodendron adhaesivum*). The relationship appears to be commensal—the shrimp benefits, while the anemone does not seem to. (The waste products produced by the crustacean may benefit its host.) This is a wonderful association to witness firsthand.

PHYLUM: Arthropoda (Arthropods).

NATIVE RANGE: Indo-Pacific.

MAXIMUM SIZE: 1 in. (2.5 cm).

MINIMUM AQUARIUM SIZE: Nano tanks, 10 gal. (38 L).

LIGHTING: Moderate to high (for host anemone).

WATER: 75-82°F (24-28°C).

FEEDING: Will scavenge meaty fish foods and likely feeds harmlessly on the protein-rich mucus of its host anemone, food particles that are trapped by the host as well as its fecal matter. It may feed on host tentacles if not fed enough.

AQUARIUM COMPATIBILITY: Needs a healthy carpet anemone host for protection and nutrition. Vulnerable to normal array of shrimp-eaters, including larger crustaceans and the usual fish suspects.

SPECIAL CARE: Acclimate slowly. Avoid abrupt shifts of salinity, pH, or temperature—fatal for most shrimps. Keep singly or in pairs.

NOTES: Do not attempt to keep commensal shrimps without a host. They typically hide and starve without an anemone. Often lives on carpet anemones and is easily recognized by the black-trimmed, bronze spots on the "tail" and white saddles on the back.

FIRE SHRIMP *Lysmata debelius*
(Blood Shrimp, Scarlet Cleaner Shrimp)

OVERVIEW: Easily the most dramatic of the many cleaner shrimps, this animal is flaming scarlet with brilliant white antennae, legs, and patches on its carapace. It commands premium prices, but is hardy and durable once acclimated to a new system. It may be more reclusive than other cleaners, although this varies from individual to individual and system to system. A mated pair may tend to feel more secure and come out in the open more often.

PHYLUM: Arthropoda (Arthropods).

NATIVE RANGE: Indo-Pacific.

MAXIMUM SIZE: 2.4 in. (6 cm).

MINIMUM AQUARIUM SIZE: 10 gal. (38 L).

LIGHTING: Dim.

WATER: 75–82°F (24–28°C).

FEEDING: Scavenger. Will eat uneaten fish food and take all sorts of meaty foods, such as mysid shrimp, and reef rations.

AQUARIUM COMPATIBILITY: Usually a good addition to a reef aquarium, although on rare occasions hungry individuals may prey on coral polyps, especially at night. Any misadventures will tend to go unnoticed in a larger tank. Actively cleans fish of parasites and necrotic tissue.

SPECIAL CARE: Needs a cave or overhanging rocky ledge for hiding. Acclimate to new water slowly over a period of an hour. Sudden changes in salinity, pH or temperature can cause instant death.

NOTES: In intensely lit reefs, the Fire Shrimp may only come out at night. Will reproduce in captivity.

HARLEQUIN SHRIMP *Hymenocera picta*
(Star-eating Shrimp)

OVERVIEW: This is a spectacular shrimp with a very specialized diet: it only feeds on sea stars. If you are willing to supply its unusual proclivity for echinoderms, this species will live a long life in captivity. The second pair of walking legs are modified into a shieldlike structure, a possible adaptation to flip sea stars over.

PHYLUM: Arthropoda (Arthropods).

NATIVE RANGE: Indo-West Pacific, Hawaii, Eastern Pacific.

MAXIMUM SIZE: 2 in. (5 cm).

MINIMUM AQUARIUM SIZE: : Nano tanks, 2 gal. (8 L).

LIGHTING: Dim.

WATER: 75–82°F (24–28°C).

FEEDING: Must provide live sea stars. Will feed on most species available in the trade and even eat pestilent *Asterina* sea stars that sometimes plague reef systems. Remove uneaten sea star pieces before they pollute the tank.

AQUARIUM COMPATIBILITY: Can be housed in a reef tank but may be more difficult to find and feed. Best in nano-reef, species aquarium. It is potential food for morays, groupers, larger dottybacks, hawkfishes, triggers, puffers, and others.

SPECIAL CARE: A very good filtration system is needed in case sea star decomposes before it is removed or eaten. Harlequin Shrimp are often available and best kept in pairs (one pair per aquarium).

NOTES: This shrimp has been known to reproduce in the aquarium. (single female can produce 200 to 5,000 eggs per month). A second species, *Hymenocera elegans*, is recognized by some.

MARBLE SHRIMP *Saron marmoratus*
(Saron Shrimp)

OVERVIEW: This genus contains a number of cryptic, nocturnal shrimps, attired with spots, lines, and reticulations, and ornate tassels. Most are shades of green and gray. The Marble Shrimp is the most often encountered. It is a known "polyp muncher," so be aware it may prey on stony corals, zoanthids, and soft coral polyps.

PHYLUM: Arthropoda (Arthropods).

NATIVE RANGE: Indo-Pacific.

MAXIMUM SIZE: 4 in. (10 cm).

MINIMUM AQUARIUM SIZE: 20 gal. (76 L).

LIGHTING: Dim.

WATER: 75–82°F (24–28°C).

FEEDING: Scavengers and carnivores. Will take mysid shrimp, adult brine shrimp, minced fish, and shrimp flesh.

AQUARIUM COMPATIBILITY: Best housed with invertebrates, other than corals and polyps, and noncrustacean eating fishes. Although often too large for smaller shrimp-eaters, large, carnivorous fishes (e.g., groupers, triggerfishes) are a threat.

SPECIAL CARE: Aggregate in the wild and can be housed in small groups in captivity. Males may fight so keep only one per tank—males have longer pinchers than females. Because they are nocturnal, provide numerous hiding places, including caves, overhangs, and deep crevices. Will spend more time in the open in a dim tank.

NOTES: The Purple-legged Saron shrimp (*Saron rectirostris*) is another genus member that is found in aquarium stores. Its care requirements are similar to *S. marmoratus*.

PEACOCK MANTIS SHRIMP *Odontodactylus scyallarus*
(Thumb-splitter Shrimp)

OVERVIEW: The notorious mantis shrimp comes out at night to hunt invertebrates and fish, but this species is so stunningly beautiful it is worthy of keeping in a tank of its own. It is has a brilliant emerald body, blue eyestalks, and a flamboyant tail tinged in scarlet. If given a cave for hiding and various shells and coral rubble, it will put on a show of underwater architecture. This species is credited with being amazingly intelligent and will come to recognize its keeper.

PHYLUM: Arthropoda (Arthropods).

NATIVE RANGE: Indo-Pacific. (Related species circumtropical).

MAXIMUM SIZE: 6 in. (15 cm).

MINIMUM AQUARIUM SIZE: 10 gal. (38 L).

LIGHTING: Dim.

WATER: 75–82°F (24–28°C).

FEEDING: Carnivore. Feed every day or two with meaty foods, including silversides, krill, pieces of marine fish, shrimp, and squid.

AQUARIUM COMPATIBILITY: Never to be trusted with other crustaceans, mollusks, or small fishes. Might be safe in a tank with larger fishes, but is best maintained in its own system, with heavy-duty filtration to handle the waste.

SPECIAL CARE: Fishermen call these "Thumb-splitter Shrimp"—they can inflict deep wounds. Handle with care. Adults can shatter the glass in a small aquarium; use an acrylic tank. Provide deep sand bed with lots of rubble.

NOTES: Specimen above is carrying a mass of eggs. Bright colors are known as "aposematic coloration" to warn predators of danger.

PEPPERMINT SHRIMP *Lysmata wurdemanni*

OVERVIEW: This attractive shrimp can be introduced into an aquarium that is plagued by the pest anemone *Aiptasia*, which can overrun a system and kill may valuable corals. It is generally nocturnal.

PHYLUM: Arthropoda (Arthropods).

NATIVE RANGE: Caribbean.

MAXIMUM SIZE: 1.75 in. (4.5 cm).

MINIMUM AQUARIUM SIZE: 10 gal. (38 L).

LIGHTING: Dim.

WATER: 75-82°F (24-28°C).

FEEDING: Carnivore. Will scavenge uneaten fish foods. Can be fed meaty fare: adult brine shrimp, mysid shrimp, reef plankton.

AQUARIUM COMPATIBILITY: *Lysmata wurdemanni* is usually a good member of a reef community. If hungry, it may steal food items from corals and anemones, causing their decline. May eat some polyps if not well fed (e.g., Yellow Polyps). Eaten by a number of fishes (including groupers, dottybacks, hawkfishes, wrasses).

SPECIAL CARE: Provide caves or rocky hiding holes in the aquascape. Best kept in small groups of three to five. May occasionally clean fishes, but not as actively as *Lysmata amboinensis* and others. Slow acclimation is essential to ensure survival.

NOTES: Many look-alike species are known and may be sold as the Peppermint Shrimp. They may or may not prey on *Aiptasia* anemones. *L. wurdemanni* has pale body with numerous horizontal stripes running from head to tail. Legs are pale orange without striping. May change color significantly over a short time, depending on its physiological condition and stress state.

SCARLET CLEANER SHRIMP *Lysmata amboinensis*
(Pacific Scarlet Cleaner Shrimp, Skunk Cleaner Shrimp)

OVERVIEW: This may be the very best of the cleaner shrimps for the beginning aquarist. It is readily available, hardy, and much less aggressive toward its own kind than the Banded or Boxer Coral Shrimps. Distinctive long, white antennae advertise its cleaning services to fishes. (The shrimp above is cleaning ectoparasites from a Yellow Tang in poor condition.)

PHYLUM: Arthropoda (Arthropods).

NATIVE RANGE: Indo-Pacific.

MAXIMUM SIZE: To about 2 in. (5 cm) long.

MINIMUM AQUARIUM SIZE: 10 gal. (38 L).

LIGHTING: Dim.

WATER: 75–82°F (24–28°C).

FEEDING: Scavenger. Will capture meaty foods missed by fishes. If target feeding, offer mysid shrimp, reef plankton, adult *Artemia*.

AQUARIUM COMPATIBILITY: These shrimp, best kept in pairs, are a great addition to any reef aquarium. Predators to avoid include groupers, dottybacks, triggerfishes, larger hawkfishes, large wrasses, and other known crustacean hunters. Especially vulnerable post-molt.

SPECIAL CARE: Acclimate slowly. Avoid any abrupt shift of salinity, pH, or temperature, which can be fatal to most shrimps. Do not overdose with iodine.

NOTES: The Caribbean version of this species is *Lysmata grabhami*, which has a pure red tail with thin white stripes on the outside edges, while *L. amboinensis* has a more complex pattern, with a central blotch of white. Regularly spawn in captivity.

SEXY SHRIMP *Thor amboinensis*
(Squat Anemone Shrimp, Ambonian Shrimp)

OVERVIEW: This is a tiny shrimp that would fit comfortably on your thumbnail. It is a hardy, wonderful little animal especially suited to small and nano aquariums without large, predatory fishes. In nature it is found living with sea anemones and large-polyped stony corals. They are fond of Bubble Corals and *Euphyllia* spp., for example. Best kept in pairs or groups of three or more. Five to seven Sexy Shrimp in a nano reef offer endless viewing opportunities. (They are called Sexy for their habit of provocatively lifting and waving their tails, as above.)

PHYLUM: Arthropoda (Arthropods).

NATIVE RANGE: Circumtropical.

MAXIMUM SIZE: 0.75 in. (2 cm).

MINIMUM AQUARIUM SIZE: Nano tanks, 2 gal. (8 L).

LIGHTING: Moderate to high (for host coral or anemone).

WATER: 75–82°F (24–28°C).

FEEDING: Will take small bits of meaty foods as fish are fed. May also feed on mucus from its host cnidarian.

AQUARIUM COMPATIBILITY: Excellent nano-aquarium species, but will often be lost in large tanks. Harmless. Preyed upon by a number of fish including anemonefishes.

SPECIAL CARE: A gregarious shrimp that lives in groups of several individuals on an anemone or coral. Should be kept in groups of three or more. Characterized by its small size, white patches, and green or tan basic color, it is easily recognizable.

NOTES: If buying sight unseen, be ready: these shrimp are small.

TIGER SNAPPING SHRIMP *Alpheus bellulus*
(Tiger Pistol Shrimp)

OVERVIEW: There are many species of snapping shrimps, so named for their ability to make a sharp *snap!* or *crack!* popping sound with their pincers. This species live in a mutually beneficial relationship with gobies (namely, members of the genera *Amblyeleotris*, *Cryptocentrus*, *Ctenogobiops,* and *Stonogobiops*) See *Reef Aquarium Fishes* (Michael, Bibliography, page 187) for more on these gobies.

PHYLUM: Arthropoda (Arthropods).

NATIVE RANGE: Circumtropical.

MAXIMUM SIZE: 3 in. (7.6 cm).

MINIMUM AQUARIUM SIZE: Nano tanks, 10 gal. (38 L).

LIGHTING: Dim.

WATER: 75–82°F (24–28°C).

FEEDING: Carnivores. Offer meaty foods for both partners: mysid shrimp, adult brine shrimp, reef plankton.

AQUARIUM COMPATIBILITY: Not all snapping shrimp associate with gobies, so make sure you get the right species. Best purchased as a fish-shrimp pair. They can be housed in pairs—males tend to be larger, with more robust pinchers. On rare occasions, will eat goby partner if the fish becomes ill or malnourished.

SPECIAL CARE: Be sure the aquarium has a deep sand bed and coral rubble for tunnel building. A piece of flat rock on the sand bed can provide a perfect roof for shrimp's burrow.

NOTES: The explosive snapping sound, audible through aquarium glass, is made by the shrimp's very large "clicker claw."

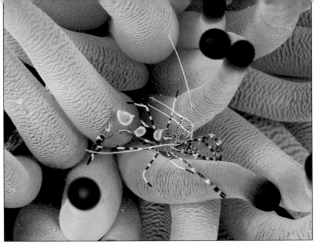

SPOTTED CLEANER SHRIMP *Periclimenes yucatanicus*
(Spotted Cleaner Shrimp)

OVERVIEW: One of the most beautiful of all shrimp, this is an incredibly delicate little invertebrate that needs the protective stinging tentacles of a sea anemone to survive in the wild. If you can keep its host alive and happy, one or more of these gems will likely thrive as well. Several similar species are sold in the aquarium trade. This species is commonly found with the Caribbean Giant Anemone (*Condylactis gigantea*).

PHYLUM: Arthropoda (Arthropods).

NATIVE RANGE: Caribbean.

MAXIMUM SIZE: 1 in. (2.5 cm).

MINIMUM AQUARIUM SIZE: Nano tanks, 10 gal. (38 L).

LIGHTING: Moderate to high (for host anemone).

WATER: 75–82°F (24–28°C).

FEEDING: Scavenges meaty foods and likely feeds harmlessly on the protein-rich mucus of its host anemone. Occasionally cleans fish alerted to the grooming services by the shrimp's swaying antennae.

AQUARIUM COMPATIBILITY: Needs a healthy anemone host for protection and nutrition. Vulnerable to predation by many carnivorous fishes. Keep one per host as they may quarrel if same sex.

SPECIAL CARE: Acclimate slowly. Avoid any abrupt shift of salinity, pH, or temperature, which can be fatal. Will also associate with *Bartholomea annulata* (see page 59).

NOTES: Similar to Pederson's Cleaner Shrimp (*Periclimenes pedersoni*) from the Caribbean—it has small purple spots and lacks the larger white saddles on the back.

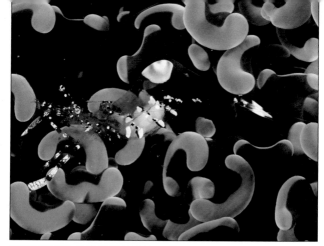

VENUSTUS COMMENSAL SHRIMP *Periclimenes venustus*
(Venustus Anemone Shrimp)

OVERVIEW: These translucent little beauties are recognized by the white patch and pinkish eyespot or ring on the abdominal hump. They have bright blue bands on their chelipeds or claw-bearing appendages. They are most commonly found with sea anemones, but may find protection by living with large-polyp stony corals, as the individual above with a Hammer Coral.

PHYLUM: Arthropoda (Arthropods).

NATIVE RANGE: West Pacific.

MAXIMUM SIZE: 1 in. (2.5 cm).

MINIMUM AQUARIUM SIZE: Nano tanks, 10 gal. (38 L).

LIGHTING: Moderate to high (for host coral or anemone).

WATER: 75–82°F (24–28°C).

FEEDING: Will scavenge meaty fish foods and likely feeds harmlessly on the protein-rich mucus of its host anemone or coral, food particles that are trapped by the host as well as its fecal matter.

AQUARIUM COMPATIBILITY: Needs a healthy coral or anemone host for protection and nutrition. Vulnerable to predation by many carnivorous fishes: dottybacks, hawkfishes, triggerfishes, large clownfishes (e.g., *Amphiprion clarkii*), wrasses, groupers, and others. May fall prey to larger crustaceans. Can be kept in small groups.

SPECIAL CARE: Acclimate slowly. Avoid abrupt shifts of salinity, pH, or temperature, which can be fatal for most shrimps. Best in peaceful nano-aquarium.

NOTES: Do not attempt to keep commensal shrimps without a host. They typically starve or fail to thrive without an anemone or coral.

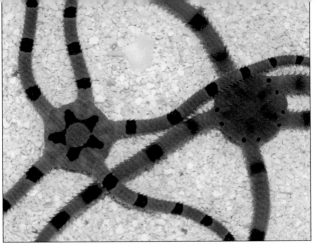

SHORT-SPINED SERPENT STAR *Ophioplocus* spp.
(Serpent Star, Banded Brittle Star)

OVERVIEW: Although they often hide in caves and under rocky ledges, most serpent stars make excellent aquarium animals, foraging uneaten food and fecal matter. Several species in this and other genera, with different colors and patterns, are available to aquarists.

PHYLUM: Echinodermata (Echinoderms).

NATIVE RANGE: Caribbean and Indo-Pacific.

MAXIMUM SIZE: 12 in. (30 cm) diameter.

MINIMUM AQUARIUM SIZE: 10 gal. (38 L).

LIGHTING: Moderate.

WATER: 75–82°F (24–28°C).

FEEDING: No direct feeding usually required if fishes are being fed. If kept in an aquarium where fish are not present, target feed once a day.

AQUARIUM COMPATIBILITY: Usually harmless, although larger species may go astray (eat polyps and small shrimps) if underfed. Regularly climb on corals, but do not cause harm.

SPECIAL CARE: Provide a rocky aquascape with places where they can hide during daylight hours.

NOTES: Their arms appear smooth or scaly, but have one or more rows of short spines running down their sides. The members of this genus have banded arms and can range from brown to pink. If they lose an arm, it will take them longer to regrow an appendage than some other serpent star genera. Can live for more than a decade in an aquarium.

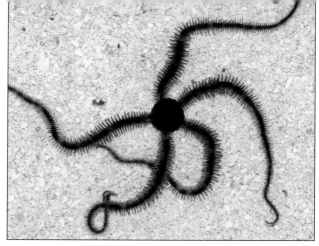

SPINY BRITTLE STAR *Ophiocoma, Ophiomastix* spp.
(Black Brittle Star, Brown Brittle Star)

OVERVIEW: A great addition to any aquarium cleanup crew, the various Brittle Stars with spiny arms do most of their work at night and hidden in the dark nooks and recesses of the aquarium, cleaning up organic waste before it can decay and cause problems.

PHYLUM: Echinodermata (Echinoderms).

NATIVE RANGE: Circumtropical.

MAXIMUM SIZE: 8 in. (20 cm) diameter.

MINIMUM AQUARIUM SIZE: 10 gal. (38 L).

LIGHTING: Moderate.

WATER: 75–82°F (24–28°C).

FEEDING: No direct feeding usually required if fishes are being fed. May extend their arms during feeding time if meaty morsels come within their reach. Targeted feeding with any sort of meaty foods (shrimp, krill, reef rations) may be necessary in an underfed reef tank.

AQUARIUM COMPATIBILITY: Generally harmless. (However, see the Green Brittle Star, aka "The Green Death," page 156.) They may be guilty of capturing small, resting fishes at night or eating soft coral polyps if underfed. In turn, certain crustaceans, such as hermit crabs and lobsters, may attack and eat them.

SPECIAL CARE: These animals do not respond well to sudden changes in water conditions and will drop their legs when stressed.

NOTES: The central disk is small in relation to the length of the five arms. Colors commonly seen are tan, gray, brown, or mottled patterns of relatively muted colors.

SAND-MOPPING CUCUMBER *Holothuria* spp.
(Donkey Dung, Edible Sea Cucumber, Tigertail Sea Cucumber)

OVERVIEW: Some people are repulsed, others curiously attracted, to sea cucumbers. These scavenging animals are primarily kept to clean and agitate the sand bed and keep it from stratifying or developing dead zones. Many different species make their way into the aquarium trade.

PHYLUM: Echinodermata (Echinoderms).

NATIVE RANGE: Circumtropical.

MAXIMUM SIZE: 16 in. (40 cm) long.

MINIMUM AQUARIUM SIZE: 50 gal. (190 L).

LIGHTING: Moderate.

WATER: 75–82°F (24–28°C).

FEEDING: Detritivore. Will take in substrate and extract anything it can digest.

AQUARIUM COMPATIBILITY: Although it carries holothurin toxins that repel attacks by predators, it is generally benign. However, if harassed by large hermit crabs, it may release toxins that can kill other tankmates. Fortunately, such disasters are rare.

SPECIAL CARE: NOTES: It is not unusual to have these cucumbers split themselves in two, an asexual form of reproduction (fission). One cucumber will go into hiding and emerge days later as two.

NOTES: *Holothuria edulis* is a common Indo-Pacific species used in Asian cooking to make "trepang" and "beche de mer." Colors vary from red and pink to tan, gray, and brown, often with a dark dorsal surface. *H. floridiana* is a common Caribbean species with a mottled gray, brown, and white pattern.

YELLOW CUCUMBER *Colochirus robustus*
(Yellow Sea Cuke)

OVERVIEW: Bright lemon-yellow color, small size, and five branching feeding arms swaying in the currents characterize this ornamental reef cucumber. It is often found in large clusters in the wild, attached to vertical stony substrates in high-current areas where particulate matter is abundant.

PHYLUM: Echinodermata (Echinoderms).

NATIVE RANGE: Indo-Pacific.

MAXIMUM SIZE: 2.3 in. (6 cm).

MINIMUM AQUARIUM SIZE: 30 gal. (114 L).

LIGHTING: Dim.

WATER: 75–82°F (24–28°C).

FEEDING: Suspension feeder. It must be fed daily with marine snow, phytoplankton, and other preparations for filter feeders. Turn off filtration and skimming equipment during feeding periods. Particulate matter in the sand bed that is put into suspension by sifting fishes (e.g., certain gobies) may also provide a source of food.

AQUARIUM COMPATIBILITY: This is a peaceful animal, but it may be seriously harassed by aggressive hermit crabs. Invertebrate-grazing fishes (e.g., angelfishes) may pick at it as well.

SPECIAL CARE: Replicate the strong currents it needs in nature. Although it resembles the body form of the much larger sea apples (*Pseudocolochirus* spp.), this species is not as likely to poison a tank with its holotoxins.

NOTES: It may reproduce by fission in the aquarium, with one animal splitting into two.

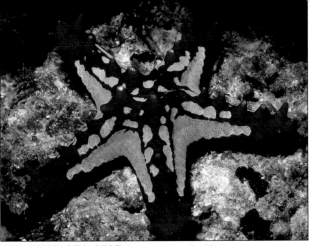

RED-KNOB SEA STAR *Protoreaster lincki*
(African Sea Star, Red-spine Sea Star)

OVERVIEW: The bright red spines of Red-knob Sea Star are brilliant, sharp, and have a network of low red ridges connecting them. While all sea stars can suffer from stress related to shipping and improper acclimation, this species is very hardy once acclimatized and a marvelous display animal.

PHYLUM: Echinodermata (Echinoderms).

NATIVE RANGE: Indo-Pacific.

MAXIMUM SIZE: 12 in. (30 cm) across (more often 7.9 in. [20 cm]).

MINIMUM AQUARIUM SIZE: 50 gal. (189 L).

LIGHTING: Moderate.

WATER: 75–82°F (24–28°C).

FEEDING: Sponge is important in its natural diet; however, It will typically accept chunks of seafood in captivity. Because this is not the most nimble of sea stars, it may have difficulty wresting food from reef decor—be sure you regularly target foods to them.

AQUARIUM COMPATIBILITY: Not suitable for reef tanks. Will eat sessile invertebrates, including anemones, zoanthid polyps, and tridacnid clams (they are less of a threat to soft and stony corals). They have been reported to capture sleeping fish tankmates.

SPECIAL CARE: May be picked on by large angelfishes and butterflyfishes. Arch enemies include triggers and pufferfishes. No invertebrate adversaries, with possible exception of large crabs.

NOTES: Slowly acclimate them, as they can suffer greatly from sudden changes in water parameters.

SPOTTED LINCKIA SEA STAR *Linckia multifora*
(Multicolored Linckia, Comet Star)

OVERVIEW: With a small size and adaptable feeding habits, this is one of the best choices of starfish for the marine aquarium. It is colorful and considerably hardier than the larger Blue Linckia (*Linckia laevigata*). It will do best in a well-established tank with live rock and sand for grazing. *Linckia multifora* is much smaller than other *Linckia*, seldom exceeding 4 in. across. It has a mottled appearance, often red, orange or yellow and white, sometimes blue.

PHYLUM: Echinodermata (Echinoderms).

NATIVE RANGE: Indo-Pacific.

MAXIMUM SIZE: 4 in. (10 cm) diameter.

MINIMUM AQUARIUM SIZE: 30 gal. (114 L).

LIGHTING: Dim.

WATER: 75–82°F (24–28°C).

FEEDING: Omnivorous. Will scavenge meaty foods, biofilms from substrates, and uneaten fish food. Offer dry pelletized or tablet foods or pieces of seafood on a feeding stick.

AQUARIUM COMPATIBILITY: Will eat ornamental sponges but is otherwise a good, non-aggressive reef tank community member. It may be harassed by certain fishes, crabs, and hermit crabs.

SPECIAL CARE: It sheds arms readily, and the lost appendage often grows into a new starfish while the "parent" regenerates its missing ray. Acclimate slowly and avoid sudden shifts of salinity.

NOTES: A Spotted Linckia is a large arm regenerating four new smaller arms at its thick end, giving the appearance of a comet and tail.

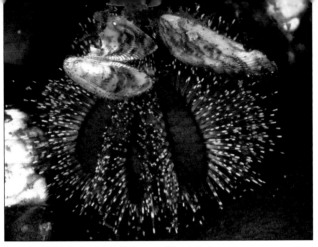

BLUE TUXEDO URCHIN *Mespilia globulus*
(Globe Urchin)

OVERVIEW: This is an especially good aquarium animal that eats nuisance filamentous algae, tends to be very hardy once it settles into a new system, and is among the most handsome of the many sea urchins. It has ten velvety blue or green wedge-shaped areas between its rows of short, very sharp spines. In most systems it will need intentional feeding of algae flakes or sheets.

PHYLUM: Echinodermata (Echinoderms).

NATIVE RANGE: West-Central Pacific.

MAXIMUM SIZE: 2 in. (5 cm) diameter.

MINIMUM AQUARIUM SIZE: 30 gal. (114 L).

LIGHTING: Moderate to bright to encourage algae growth.

WATER: 75-82°F (24-28°C).

FEEDING: Omnivore. Will graze on algae and also scavenge uneaten foods. If algae crop is limited, offer it herbivore foods or nori strips and minced seafood or marine fish flesh several times per week.

AQUARIUM COMPATIBILITY: Generally a welcome addition to most aquariums. May attack certain soft corals (e.g., *Xenia*).

SPECIAL CARE: Like some other urchins, this species accumulates bits of seaweed, coral rubble, shells, and other reef debris on its spines to camouflage it from predators. Most healthy animals will have a collection of found materials on their spine tips; specimens that have dropped their defenses may be stressed, starving, or in poor health.

NOTES: Always acclimate a new urchin slowly and avoid sudden changes of salinity, temperature, pH, and alkalinity.

SEA EGG *Tripneustes* spp.
(Collector Sea Urchin, Preacher's Cap Urchin)

OVERVIEW: These are creatures of seagrass beds, and they will do well in the aquarium. While they prefer large expanses of open sand and planted seagrasses, they will live in a conventional reef tank. To enhance their camouflage, they will carry bits of debris, shells, seagrass, thermometers, etc., with their pedicellariae. They are proficient algivores that will graze algae, even the more noxious types.

PHYLUM: Echinodermata (Echinoderms).

NATIVE RANGE: Circumtropical.

MAXIMUM SIZE: 4 in. (10 cm).

MINIMUM AQUARIUM SIZE: 50 gal. (190 L).

LIGHTING: Moderate to bright—enough to encourage algae growth.

WATER: 75–82°F (24–28°C).

FEEDING: Primarily herbivorous; forage on detritus and will take meaty foods. These urchins love Japanese nori seaweed.

AQUARIUM COMPATIBILITY: Can be housed in reef aquarium, although may knock over or carry around coral/zoanthid colonies. If underfed, may also eat soft coral polyps (for example, *Xenia*), but usually behaves. Do not keep with toadfishes, triggers, puffers, or porcupinefishes.

SPECIAL CARE: Venomous pedicellariae (tube feet) can give a painful, but not deadly, nip—handle with care.

NOTES: Like all echinoderms, Sea Eggs must be acclimated carefully and given stable conditions without abrupt shifts of salinity or pH. Colors vary considerably. The West Indian Sea Egg (*Tripneustes ventricosus*) may be red, black, or dark purple with short white spines.

The big, the bad & the unlikely to survive

There is no doubt that we are much better equipped to take care of marine invertebrates now than any time in the history of the aquarium hobby. New technology, much-improved water conditions, a wide range of food types, and a glut of good information has accounted for our current success. It was not so long ago that the idea of successfully keeping stony corals alive in the aquarium, let alone having them grow and be harvested for resale, was a pipe dream. While we certainly have made amazing advances, there are still animals that are best left in the wild, however.

Many of the animals covered in this section are simply too difficult to keep for the average or even accomplished aquarist. They may not ship well, suffering from the stress associated with the long trip from the reef to the aquarium store. Some have special nutritional needs that are difficult to meet and others naturally have very short life spans. There are also species that live in much cooler water than we maintain in our aquariums. If placed in warmer water, they will live abbreviated lives.

Some of the species included here are dangerous to their tankmates or even to hobbyists. The genera of cephalopods known as the "blue-ringed" octopuses, for example, have a potentially lethal bite. I know people who have had first-hand experience with the blue-ring bite and I can tell you it is not worth the risk. (In one case, the individual stopped breathing if he fell asleep and had to be kept awake for two days. The effects of the neurotoxin on his health lasted for more than six months.) There are species that will poison fish tankmates if they die or are greatly stressed. There are also species that are so rare or so ecologically important in the wild that encouraging collection is irresponsible.

Granted, we continue to make advances in the care of some of the species in this section. For example, there are advanced hobbyists continually attempting to unravel the feeding and care requirements of the hard-to-sustain large-polyp stony corals in the genera *Alveopora* and *Goniopora*. But while seasoned aquarists may disagree with my inclusion of one or more species, the inverts listed are not good choices for the vast majority of marine hobbyists.

MAGNIFICENT SEA ANEMONE *Heteractis magnifica*
This a large, glorious animal that seldom settles down and survives in the aquarium. It will move around a tank restlessly until it wastes away. This a species that ought not be collected from the reef. The captive-propagated Bubble-tip Anemone is a much better choice.

CORKSCREW ANEMONE *Macrodactyla doreensis*
This species rarely thrives in captivity and requires regular feeding and expert care. Other hard-to-keep species: Leathery Anemone (*Heteractis crispa*), Adhesive or Pizza Anemone (*Cryptodendron adhaesivum*), and Giant Carpet Anemone (*Stichodactyla gigantea*).

TUBE ANEMONES *Cerianthus* spp.

Dramatically beautiful, these animals often prove disastrous for aquarists when their powerful stinging tentacles start to kill corals, *Tridacna* clams, and even fishes. They are best maintained in a species tank where they can be treated as the centerpiece.

GREEN BRITTLE STAR *Ophiarachna incrassata*

Nicknamed "The Green Death," this stealthy hunter is commonly blamed for the disappearance of small fishes that it hunts and captures when they are resting at night. Will also eat ornamental shrimp and crabs. Best avoided or kept only with large, robust tankmates.

CARNATION CORAL *Dendronephthya* spp.
A heartbreak group for reef aquarists, these magnificent soft corals have poorly understood feeding requirements. They demand customized circulation and phytoplankton feeding systems and almost never survive long, even in the best of reef aquarium conditions.

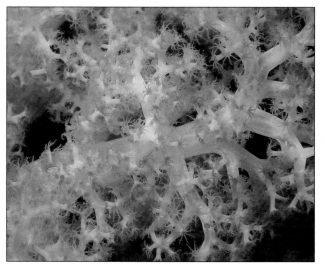

COLORED TREE CORAL *Scleronephthya* spp.
Like *Dendronephthya*, the captive care and feeding of these glorious soft corals is still being studied and is far from perfected. They typically live for a short time in the aquarium and virtually always waste away within a period of weeks.

FLOWERPOT CORAL *Goniopora djiboutiensis*

The feeding of these eye-catching corals remains a challenge, and most slowly lose strength and tissue, perishing within a year of purchase. Feeding a variety of live and prepared zooplankton and phytoplankton seems to improve success rates. For experts only.

YELLOW SUN CORAL *Tubastrea aurea*

These are stunning corals, but too many aquarists buy them not realizing that they need daily targeted feedings of meaty zooplankton foods. With proper care they can do very well and will often spread throughout the system. Study their requirements before buying.

HAIRY-LEGGED HERMIT CRABS *Dardanus* spp.
A great many hermit crabs, this genus especially, that make their way into aquarium shops can grow large and will not hesitate to prey on corals, anemones, other crabs, clams, plants, and even inactive fishes in the dark. Keep with large, rugged tankmates only.

HORSESHOE CRABS *Limulus polyphemus*, others
Holdovers from prehistoric times, these fascinating bottom dwellers need large aquariums with broad expanses of open sand bed and targeted feeding. In a typical reef aquarium they tend to starve or get themselves fatally wedged into tight spots in the aquascape.

SALLY LIGHTFOOT CRAB *Percnon gibbesi*
Although handsome and interesting to watch, these lightning-fast hunters have few friends among aquarists who have kept them. They get progressively more predatory as they grow and will unhesitatingly attack and kill other crabs, shrimp, anemones, clams, and fishes.

SPIDER DECORATOR CRAB *Camposia retusa*
The various decorator crabs disguise themselves by covering themselves with living sponges, tunicates, macroalgae, and soft corals. They can decimate a reef tank and are predatory on other invertebrates. They do make fascinating subjects if kept in a species tank.

FEATHER STAR *Crinoidea* spp.

Often flamboyantly colorful, the Feather Stars are related to the sea stars and urchins, but are virtually impossible to keep alive in captivity. They are filter feeders and exceptionally selective about what they eat. When dying, their arms break free as they disintegrate.

LETTUCE SLUG *Elysia crispata*

Similar to the nudibranchs, these Caribbean mollusks are somewhat easier to keep. Beautiful and quite active as they forage on live macroalgae, they unfortunately need more grazing opportunities than most aquarists can provide and tend to be very short-lived.

MACROALGAE • INVASIVE SPECIES

CAULERPA *Caulerpa taxifolia*

Smothering 30,000 square acres of the Mediterranean after escaping from the Monaco Aquarium, a cold-hardy strain of *Caulerpa taxifolia* is now classed as a Federal Noxious Weed in the U.S. Fines of up to $10,000 for possession are in place in California.

MUSHROOM POLYP • PREDATORY

ELEPHANT EAR MUSHROOM *Amplexidiscus fenestrafer*

A corallimorph that grows up to 18 inches (46 cm), this is a highly carnivorous animal that mimics anemones to catch unsuspecting fishes in its closable, purse-like oral disk. Clownfishes are especially susceptible. Makes an interesting specimen in a species tank.

FISH-KILLING NUDIBRANCH *Phyllidia varicosa*
The culprit behind numerous mass killings of aquarium fish collections, this exceptionally beautiful sea slug possesses a deadly toxin in its slime coat. If it is wounded or dies in an aquarium (starvation is common), the dying animal can take all your fishes with it.

NUDIBRANCH *Phyllodesmium, Flabellina, Chromodoris,* **others**
The often astonishing colors and shapes of these many species of shell-less snails may serve to signal would-be predators of their toxic nature. Aquarists, too, should be warned off: they have highly specialized feeding habits and typically perish quickly in captivity.

BLUE-RING OCTOPUS *Hapalochlaena lunulata*
Here is a diminutive reef animal with a long history of killing humans, mostly fisherfolk in tropical countries. The animal pictured carries enough toxin to kill 26 people. Death comes through paralysis and suffocation. Do not buy these potentially deadly animals.

SEA APPLE *Pseudocolochirus* spp.
A gaudy animal commonly sold in the aquarium trade, this glorified sea cucumber is a filter feeder that virtually always starves slowly in captivity. If wounded, threatened, or dying, it can release toxins that have wiped out countless aquarium fishes and invertebrates.

164

SEA PEN *Cavernularia* spp.

These solitary soft corals can make very attractive and interesting aquarium subjects, but they have demands that most hobbyists cannot meet: a very deep (8-24 inches or 20-60 cm) bed of soft substrate and targeted feedings of a variety of planktonic foods.

SEA STARS *Protoreaster, Oreaster, Fromia, Linckia,* others

Most marine aquarists have tried to keep sea stars, but they tend to suffer shipping stresses, then succumb to bacterial infections. Some species feed on sponge, and these slowly perish of starvation. The best choice for beginners is the Spotted Linckia (page 151).

CROWN-OF-THORNS *Acanthaster planci*
Here is a formidable creature, growing to 18 inches (46 cm) and covered in long, razor-sharp, venom-tipped spines. It eats coral polyps in the wild and will ravage a reef aquarium. Aquarists who have been stung report that the pain persists for many hours.

CATALINA PEPPERMINT SHRIMP *Lysmata californicus*
Unscrupulous collectors are known to sell these cool-water animals into the aquarium trade, where hobbyists buy them not knowing that they cannot tolerate warm temperatures for extended periods. For tanks kept below 60°F (16°C) only. Will not eat *Aiptasia*.

BUMBLEBEE SNAIL *Engina mendicaria*
These are among the prettiest little snails sold to aquarists, but they are carnivores that will ignore algae and instead hunt polychaete worms and other snails. They will scavenge some meaty detritus, but on balance may be a negative addition to a reef aquarium.

CONE SHELLS *Conus geographus*, *Conus striatus*, others
Conus is the largest marine invertebrate genus, with 500 living species. It is also the deadliest: many species have a venom-injecting proboscis designed to sting and paralyze fish almost instantly. Human victims can suffer blindness, paralysis, and heart failure.

FLAMINGO TONGUE *Cyphoma gibbosum*
Sometimes known as Leopard Conchs, these eye-catching Caribbean snails feed exclusively on the polyps and flesh of live corals, primarily gorgonians. Feeding them properly in the aquarium is a virtual impossibility. They are best viewed in the wild.

MARGARITA SNAILS *Tegula funebralis*
Native to the Pacific coast of North America, these active herbivores are appropriate only for cool-water marine aquariums. In a typical tropical tank they slowly lose strength and perish—a shameful waste of an animal capable of living up to a century in the wild.

TRITON'S TRUMPHET *Charonia* spp.
Capable of attacking and devouring Crown-of-Thorns Starfish as well as sea urchins, this snail is potentially too large (up to 24 inches or 60 cm) and predatory for the aquarium. It has a toxic saliva and will eat resting fishes at night. It should be left on the reef.

SPONGES *Clathria*, *Haliclona*, *Aplysina*, many others
Undeniably attractive, many colorful sponges are available to aquarists. Most do poorly in the average aquarium, where they fail to find sufficient foods to filter out of the water column. Never buy a sponge without first studying its captive care and feeding requirements.

SPANISH DANCER *Hexabranchus sanguineus*
Among the largest dorid nudibranchs, Spanish Dancers are brilliantly colored and put on a spectacular show when swimming in the water column. Their size (up to 24 inches or 60 cm) and diet of live sponges make them very poor candidates for most home aquariums.

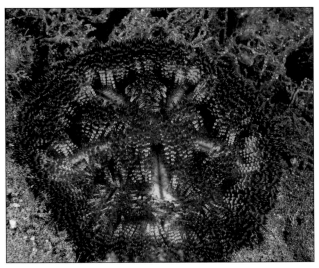

FIRE URCHINS *Asthenosoma* spp.
Vivid colors in invertebrates often serve to warn away predators. The various species sold as Fire Urchins can severely sting humans, causing long-lasting, excruciating pain or even shock. Not recommended for the average aquarist or a tank within reach of children.

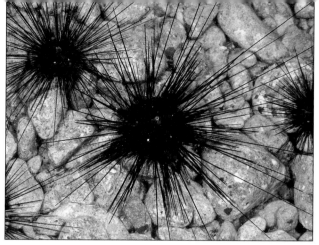

LONGSPINED SEA URCHIN *Diadema antillarum, D. setosum*
These are fascinating animals to observe, but they require large aquariums with expanses of open substrate. In a small tank they tend to be destructive and short-lived, while posing a threat to the aquarist with the ability to inflict very painful stings if contacted.

SLATE PENCIL URCHIN *Heterocentrotus* spp.
Pencil Urchins are curious creatures that tend to bulldoze their way through most reef aquariums, tumbling rock, dislodging corals, and generally making a nuisance of themselves. They are appropriate for a species tank or aquarium with a well-anchored aquascape.

171

The 10 fish groups most dangerous to invertebrates

The members of the families listed below have diets that include a variety of different invertebrates prized by reef aquarists, and they will definitely bring these predatory behaviors into the home aquarium. However, there are exceptions to the general rule in some of these families. For example, there are a handful of triggerfishes that eat zooplankton (e.g., the Sargassum Triggerfish, *Xanthichthys ringens*) and can be housed with many different invertebrates.

1. Triggerfishes: Most members of this genus have diets that include worms, mollusks, crustaceans, and echinoderms. Some will also bite the tips off of stony coral colonies.

2. Pufferfishes: These polyphagous fishes have some of the most indiscriminately omnivorous feeding habits of all reef fishes, eating sponges, corals, mollusks, worms, crustaceans, and echinoderms.

3. Porcupinefishes: These fish regularly eat mollusks, crustaceans, and sea urchins.

4. Large Wrasses: There are a number of wrasse genera, including the *Bodianus*, *Coris*, *Cheilinus*, *Halichoeres*, *Hemigymnus*, *Hologymnosus*, *Gomphosus*, *Novaculichthys*, *Oxycheilinus*, and *Thalassoma*, that cannot be trusted with snails, small clams, ornamental worms, shrimps, crabs, and small sea urchins. Research any wrasse species of interest before adding it to your invertebrate aquarium.

5. Moray Eels: There are many morays that will hunt and eat crustaceans; some also eat sea urchins.

6. Groupers: Although not a threat to sessile/encrusting invertebrates, there are many species that will eat crustaceans.

7. Hawkfishes: The larger members of this family are especially deadly hunters of crustaceans, and some will eat small brittle stars. Even the smaller, more popular hawkfishes will sometimes "go astray" and nail a newly added shrimp or crab.

8. Butterflyfishes: While not a threat to ornamental crustaceans, many of these fishes dine on coral polyps, anemones, and ornamental worms.

9. Spade or Batfishes: These larger fishes are known to eat a variety of different sedentary invertebrates, including sea anemones and soft corals.

10. Large Angelfishes: A number of larger angelfishes (e.g., genus *Holacanthus* and *Pomacanthus*) will eat some soft corals, large-polyped stony corals, and may nip *Tridacna* clam mantles.

2-Gallon (8 L) Nano-Reef Aquarium

3 Zoanthid colonies	*Zoanthus/Palythoa* spp.
3 Mushroom Anemone colonies	*Discosoma/Rhodactis* spp.
3 Astraea Snails	*Astraea/Lithopoma* spp.
1 Boxer Crab	*Lybia tesselata*

There are some animals that are better suited to a nano-aquarium. This is the case for the relatively cryptic Boxer Crab. This fascinating animal is worth keeping because of its sea anemone partnership and its ornate coloration. Provide a small cave using rubble and rock whose central cavity can be viewed from the front of the tank. Place cnidarian colonies on the rock structure. Do not house with other crabs. A nano-goby or two would provide some fish action.

*Boxer Crab (*Lybia tesselata*): note small anemone "pom poms."*

*Zoanthid colony (*Zoanthus* spp.): colorful and easy to keep.*

173

5-Gallon (19 L) Nano-Reef Aquarium

3 Zoanthid colonies	*Zoanthus/Palythoa* spp.
3 Mushroom Anemone colonies	*Discosoma/Rhodactis* spp.
3 Astraea Snails	*Astraea/Lithopoma* spp.
2 Scarlet Hermit Crabs	*Paguristes cadenati*
Pair Harlequin Shrimp	*Hymenocera picta*

Here is a display that highlights the most flamboyantly pigmented of all the crustaceans—the Harlequin Shrimp. It eats only the tube feet and arms of sea stars, which you must provide at about one per week. Any sea star will do, including the ubiquitous Chocolate Chip Sea Star. Add a firefish or goby to complete the community.

Harlequin Shrimp can be kept in pairs or groups. Colors vary considerably, and females are often larger than their mates.

10-Gallon (38 L) House of Hermit

1 Yellow Hairy Hermit Crab   *Aniculus maximus*

This character is very destructive but a worthy aquarium resident! It cannot be trusted with other inverts; thus, it is best housed in a small species tank. Larger members of the genus *Dardanus* would be good substitutes, although the Yellow Hairy is the most spectacular hermit of them all. Provide plenty of larger, empty shells for this crab when upsizing is necessary. Use rock and sand as decor elements.

*Yellow Hairy Hermit Crab (*Aniculus maximus*): a prized hermit crab species, best and observed kept in its own small display aquarium.*

12-Gallon (45 L) Fastest Claw in the West (Pacific)

3 Astraea Snails	*Astraea/Lithopoma* spp.
2 Scarlet Hermit Crabs	*Paguristes cadenati*
1 Tiger Snapping Shrimp	*Alpheus bellulus*
1 Shrimp Goby (or pair)	*Cryptocentrus* spp.

This little reef features the fascinating relationship that occurs between the Tiger Snapping Shrimp (*Alpheus bellulus*) and a goby partner. (If you can acquire a goby pair, that is even better.) Provide a deep sand bed with bits of shell and rubble. Add a Purple Firefish (*Nemateleotris decora*) for color and behavior. Listen for the popping shots produced by the pistol-like claw of the *Alpheus*!

The centerpiece of this aquarium is Tiger Snapping Shrimp with its commensal goby, or goby pair—in this case the Yellow Shrimp Goby.

20-Gallon (45 L) Fire Shrimp and Soft Corals

4 Zoanthid colonies	*Zoanthus/Palythoa* spp.
1 Umbrella Leather	*Coral Sarcophyton* spp.
1 Kenya Tree	*Capnella* spp.
2 Xenia colonies	*Xenia* spp.
2 Australian Lord	*Acanthastrea lordhowensis*
2 Banded Trochus Snails	*Trochus* spp.
Pair Fire Shrimp	*Lysmata debelius*
1 Blue-legged Hermit Crab	*Clibanarius tricolor*
2 Scarlet Hermit Crabs	*Paguristes cadenati*
2 Yellow Cucumbers	*Colochirus robustus*

A nice soft coral combo, with a striking pair of Fire Shrimp. However, the real "eye candy" are the *Acanthastrea* colonies, which are available in amazing colors (place near bottom away from soft corals). The Yellow Cucumbers add color and interest. Acquire small soft coral colonies and have your pruning shears ready! Provide a mound of coral rock with at least one cave or ledge where the Fire Shrimp can find refuge and security. Skimming and carbon should be employed to keep soft coral toxins in check. Potential fish additions would include perchlets, demoiselles, gobies, and firefishes. Don't overstock, as smaller tanks require careful feeding and water quality management.

*A mated pair of Fire Shrimp (*Lysmata debelius*): white antennae advertise their cleaning services to fish in the community.*

30-Gallon (114 L) Shrimp-Sea Star Combo Platter

Fighting Conch	*Strombus alatus*
Pair Marbled Saron Shrimp	*Saron marmoratus*
3 Electric Blue Hermit Crabs	*Calcinus elegans*
Redknob Sea Star	*Protoreaster linckii*

This is an unusual tank that featured to "bad boys" that are not welcome in the reef tank, but worthy pets. Use live rock to create two patch reefs with caves (the home of the Saron Shrimps). The rest of the tank should be an unobstructed sand bed—this is sea star habitat. The hermits are enlisted for scavenger duties, while the Fighting Conch will help stir the substrate.

*The Red-knob Sea Star (*Protoreaster linckii*) is a showstopper animal that will require an open expanse of sand and targeted feeding.*

55-Gallon (209 L) Bullet-proof Cnidarian Aquarium

2 Clavularia colonies	*Clavularia* spp.
1 Green Star Polyps	*Briarium* spp.
1 Cabbage Coral	*Sinularia* spp.
1 Tree Coral	*Litophyton* spp.
3 Zoanthid colonies	*Zoanthus/Protopalythoa*
1 Yellow Polyps	*"Parazoanthus gracilis"*
1 Moon Coral	*Favia* sp.
2 Scarlet Cleaner Shrimp	*Lysmata amboinensis*
4 Blue-legged Hermit Crab	*Clibanarius tricolor*
1 Cone Shell Hermit Crab	*Ciliopagurus strigatus*
5 Star Snails	*Astraea/Lithopoma* spp.
4 Short-spined Serpent Stars	*Ophioderma* sp.

While a lovely example of a reef garden, this community also includes some of the most durable soft corals and colonial polyps available to aquarists from the phylum Cnidaria. A *Favia* sp. Moon Coral would make for a hardy stony coral centerpiece. Most are zooxanthellae-bearing members of the group, so moderate to bright light will ensure happy polyps. A handful of algae-eating hermits and snails, as well as the mega-scavenging brittle stars are included. Perchlets, chromis, demoiselles, gobies, firefishes would all be good fish choices.

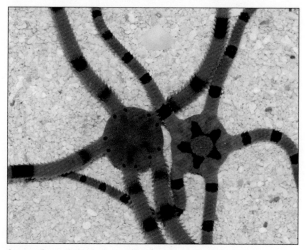

Serpent Stars (Ophioderma spp.) are easy-to-keep scavengers that add biological balance and interest to any invertebrate aquarium.

75-Gallon (285 L) Large-polyped Lobster Lagoon

3 Zoanthid colonies	*Zoanthus/Protopalythoa*
4 Mushroom anemone colonies	*Discosoma/Rhodactis* spp.
3 Australian Lord	*Acanthastrea lordhowensis*
2 Candy Cane Coral	*Caulastrea* spp.
3 Cat's Eye Corals	*Cynarina/Scolymia* spp.
2 Open Brain Coral	*Trachyphyllia geoffroyi*
1 "Wellsophyllia" Coral	*Trachyphyllia radiata*
8 Banded Trochus Snails	*Trochus* spp.
4 Scarlet Hermit Crabs	*Paguristes cadenati*
6 Zebra Reef Hermit Crabs	*Calcinus seurati*
1 Reef Lobster	*Enoplometopus debelius*
4 Short-spined Serpent Stars	*Ophioderma* spp.
2 Sea Cucumbers	*Holothuria* spp.

This colorful community represents an Indo-Pacific mud/sand lagoon. Keep everything in moderation with this tank: moderate water movement is appreciated more than stronger, direct currents, while moderate light levels will keep these corals healthy. Keep over half of the aquarium bottom rock-free. Fishes might include perchlets, anthias, dottybacks, cardinalfishes, fairy wrasses, gobies, dartfishes, sand-sifting gobies and/or jawfishes.

*Purple Reef Lobster (*Enoplometopus debelius*): a prize species among the small reef lobsters. Keep singly to avoid cannibalism.*

75-Gallon (285 L) Clam Paradise

3 Xenia colonies	*Xenia* spp.
2 Umbrella Leather Corals	*Sarcophyton* spp.
1 Finger Leather	*Sinularia* spp.
1 Rasta Leather Coral	*Sinularia flexibilis*
3 Ricordea	*Ricordea floridea*
1 Bubble Coral	*Plerogyra sinuosa*
2 Montipora	*Montipora* spp.
1 Derasa Clam	*Tridacna derasa*
1 Squamosa Clam	*Tridacna squamosa*
8 Banded Trochus Snail	*Trochus* spp.
1 Emerald Crab	*Mithraculus sculptus*
8 Scarlet Hermit Crab	*Paguristes cadenati*
5 Peppermint Shrimp	*Lysmata* sp.

This tridacnid habitat is reminiscent of shallow reef face habitats in the West Pacific (except for the *Ricordea floridea*). Place these clams on the sand bottom or on a patch of rubble. In this way, they will be easier to relocate if necessary. Bright lights (metal halide or T8s) are a must. Remember to leave plenty of room around the clams for growth. Clam-safe fishes would include anthias, perchlets, reef basslets, dottybacks, most damselfishes, small wrasses, gobies, and firefishes.

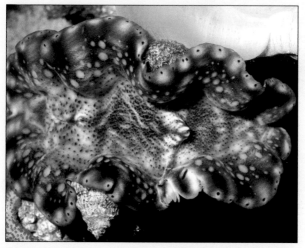

Clam breeders are producing some spectacular color morphs of the easy-to-keep Tridacna derasa *clam, shown, as well as* T. squamosa.

75-Gallon (285 L) Clown Condo

3 Clove Polyps	*Clavularia* spp.
3 Green Star Polyps	*Briareum* sp.
1 Mumps Coral	*Lobophytum* spp.
2 Tree Coral	*Litophyton* spp.
1 Finger Leather	*Sinularia* spp.
1 Bubble-tip Sea Anemone	*Entacmaea quadricolor*
1 Emerald Crab	*Mithraculus sculptus*
7 Blue-legged Hermit Crab	*Clibanarius tricolor*
5 Star Snails	*Astraea/Lithopoma* spp.
4 Brittle Stars	*Ophioderma* spp.
1 Sea Egg	*Tripneustes gratilla*
1 Pair Maroon Anemonefish	*Premnas biaculeatus*

Not only are they colorful, anemonefishes wallowing among the stinging tentacles of their sea anemone host is something to behold! Place one or several smaller Bubble-tip Sea Anemones in the aquarium, which should have moderate to bright lighting and a couple of live rock patch reefs for the anemones to adhere to and hide in. Add a captive-raised pair of anemonefish. Also include a variety of soft corals, both matt and tree varieties for interest. The Sea Egg is included for algae control and interest—it will collect debris to increase camouflage.

Maroon Anemonefish pairs feature a big, fiesty female and a small, dutiful male. They will readily accept a Bubble-tip Sea Anemone.

180-Gallon (684 L) SPS Garden

12 Acropora colonies	*Acropora* spp.
3 Hedgehog Coral	*Echinophyllia* spp.
3 Brain Coral	*Favites* spp.
2 Lobed Brain Coral	*Lobophyllia hemprichii*
3 Moon Coral	*Favia* spp.
3 Bird Nest Coral	*Seriatopora* spp.
4 Montipora colonies	*Montipora* spp.
2 Cauliflower Coral	*Pocillopora damicornis*
1 Squamosa Clam	*Tridacna squamosa*
20 Banded Trochus Snail	*Trochus* spp.
1 Coco Worm	*Protula* sp.
3 Giant Feather Dusters	*Sabellastarte* spp.
1 Emerald Crab	*Mithraculus sculptus*
10 Blue-leg Hermit Crab	*Clibanarius tricolor*
4 Electric Blue Hermit Crab	*Calcinus elegans*
2 Scarlet Cleaner Shrimp	*Lysmata amboinensis*
2 Fire Shrimp	*Lysmata debelius*
8 Short-spined Serpent Star	*Ophioderma* sp.

This is the neophyte reefkeeper's dream tank. A beautiful variety of small-polyped stony corals, a few large-polyped stony corals mixed in, with a lively community of colorful fishes. These animals require a more advanced aquarium system (the best lighting, calcium reactor or frequent manual additions of calcium supplements, great water movement). The fish community could include anthias, dottybacks, cardinalfishes, small hawkfishes, chromis, demoiselles, fairy wrasses, other small reef-safe wrasses, a tang, and a rabbitfish.

Acropora sp.: aquacultured colonies are making the keeping of these classic reefbuilding staghorn corals increasingly possible. (ORA)

SCIENTIFIC NAME INDEX

[SPECIES TO AVOID IN RED]

References & Suggested Reading

Borneman, E. H. 2001. *Aquarium Corals: Selection, Husbandry and Natural History*. T.F.H. Publications, Inc., Neptune City, N.J. 464 pp.

Calfo, A. and R. Fenner. 2003. *Reef Invertebrates, an Essential Guide to Selection, Care and Compatibility*. Reading Trees and Wet Web Media Publications, Monroeville, Pa. 398 pp.

Fosså, S., and A. J. Nilsen. 1996–. *The Modern Coral Reef Aquarium*. Birgit Schmettkamp Verlag, Germany.

Gosliner, T.M., D.W. Behrens, and G.C. Williams. 1996. *Coral Reef Animals of the Indo-Pacific*. Sea Challengers, Monterey, Calif. 314 pp.

Humann, P. 1992. *Reef Creature Identification, Florida, Caribbean, Bahamas*. New World Publications, Inc., Jacksonville, Fla. 320 pp.

Humann, P. 1993. *Reef Coral Identification, Florida, Caribbean, Bahamas, including Marine Plants*. New World Publications, Inc., Jacksonville, Fla. 239 pp.

Michael, S. W. 2005. *A PocketExpert Guide: Reef Aquarium Fishes*, Microcosm/T.F.H. Professional Series. T.F.H. Publications, Inc., Neptune City, N.J. 448 pp.

Ruppert, E. F., and R. D. Barnes. 1994. *Invertebrate Zoology*. Saunders College Publishing, Ft. Worth, Texas. 1056 pp.

Shimek, R. L. 2004. *Marine Invertebrates: 500+ Essential-To-Know Aquarium Species*. T.F.H. Publications, Inc., Neptune City, N.J. 448 pp.

Sprung, J. 1999. *Corals: A Quick Reference Guide*. Ricordea Publishing, Coconut Grove, Fla. 240 pp.

Veron, J., M. Stafford-Smith. 2000. *Corals of the World, Volume 1*. Australian Institute of Marine Sciences, Townsville. 463 pp.

COMMON NAME INDEX

[SPECIES TO AVOID IN RED]

COMMON NAME INDEX

PHOTOGRAPHY

All photographs by SCOTT W. MICHAEL except where indicated:

Matthew L. Wittenrich: 14, 21, 29, 52, 62, 63 (T, B), 72, 73 (T)), 76, 84, 98, 102, 103, 118, 121, 125, 126, 129, 133 (T), 136, 140, 159 (B), 160, 164 (B), 167 (T), 171, 172 (T), 174 (B), 175, 177, 178, 180, 184, 185. Front Cover; Back Cover (T, M).

Janine Cairns-Michael (coralrealm.com): 12, 16, 17, 18, 26, 42 (T, B), 47, 54 (B), 56, 78, 79 (T), 87, 89 (B), 90, 91 (T, B), 95 (T), 96, 99, 101, 107, 144, 151, 156 (T), 157 (B), 158 (B), 161 (T, B), 166 (T), 170 (B), 171 (T).

Alf Jacob Nilsen (Bioquatic Photo: biophoto.net): 38, 45, 48, 50, 51, 53, 66, 68, 69, 71, 77, 81, 93, 122, 130, 137, 141, 142, 156 (B), 159 (T), 162 (T), 165 (T, B), 177.

David Burr, Vivid Aquariums (vividaquariums.com): 73 (B), 74, 75 (T, B), 85, 88, 89 (T).

Paul Humann (fishid.com): 45, 58, 110, 169 (T).

Robert M. Fenner (wetwebmedia.com): 57.

Larry Jackson: 95 (B).

NOAA (Steve Lonhart (SIMoN / MBNMS): 168 (B).

Denise Nielsen Tackett (tackettproductions.com): 167 (B).

DESIGN
Linda Provost

COLOR
Digital Engine (Burlington, VT)

EDITING
Judith Billard, Janice Heilmann, James Lawrence, Emily Stetson, John Sweeney, Mary E. Sweeney

Scott W. Michael is an internationally recognized writer, underwater photographer, and marine biology researcher specializing in reef fishes. He is a regular contributor to *Aquarium Fish* magazine and is the author of the *PocketExpert Guide to Marine Fishes* (Microcosm/T.F.H.), the 6-volume *Reef Fishes* Series (Microcosm/T.F.H.), *Reef Sharks & Rays of the World* (Sea Challengers), and *Aquarium Sharks & Rays* (Microcosm/T.F.H.).

Having studied biology at the University of Nebraska, he has been involved in research projects on sharks, rays, frogfishes, and the behavior of reef fishes. He has also served as scientific consultant for National Geographic Explorer and the Discovery Channel. His work has led him from Cocos Island in the Eastern Pacific to various points in the Indo-Pacific as well as the Red Sea, the Gulf of Mexico, and many Caribbean reefs.

A marine aquarist since boyhood, he has kept tropical fishes for more than 30 years, with many years of involvement in the aquarium world, including a period of tropical fish store management and ownership. He is a partner in an extensive educational website, www.coralrealm.com.

Scott Michael lives with his wife, underwater photographer Janine Cairns-Michael, and their Golden Retriever, Ruby, in Lincoln, Nebraska.